Probation and Parole

Probation and Parole

Compiled and Edited by

BARBARA A. KAY, Ph.D.
Assistant Professor of Sociology and Anthropology
University of Massachusetts
Amherst, Massachusetts

and

CLYDE B. VEDDER, Ph.D.
Professor of Sociology and Anthropology
Northern Illinois University
DeKalb, Illinois

CHARLES C THOMAS · PUBLISHER
Springfield · Illinois · U.S.A.

Published and Distributed Throughout the World by
CHARLES C THOMAS • PUBLISHER
BANNERSTONE HOUSE
301-327 East Lawrence Avenue, Springfield, Illinois, U.S.A.

*With THOMAS BOOKS careful attention is given to all details of
manufacturing and design. It is the Publisher's desire to present books
that are satisfactory as to their physical qualities and artistic possibilities and appropriate for their particular use. THOMAS BOOKS will
be true to those laws of quality that assure a good name and good will.*

Printed in the United States of America
N-1

CONTRIBUTORS

NAT R. ARLUKE, *Senior Officer in Charge, District No. 7, Bureau of Parole, New Jersey Department of Institutions and Agencies.*

CHESTER H. BARTOO, *Senior Deputy Probation Officer, Central Adult Investigation, Los Angeles County Probation Department, California.*

RALPH W. ENGLAND, JR., *Chairman, Department of Sociology, University of Rhode Island, Kingston, Rhode Island.*

VICTOR H. EVJEN, *Assistant Chief of Probation, Administrative Office of the United States.*

EDMOND FITZGERALD, *Chief Probation Officer, Kings County Court, Brooklyn, New York.*

J. DOUGLAS GRANT, *Chief Research Division, California Department of Corrections.*

BARBARA KAY, *Department of Sociology and Anthropology, University of Massachusetts, Amherst, Massachusetts.*

PETER P. LEJINS, *Professor of Sociology, University of Maryland, College Park, Maryland.*

ALFRED MURRAH, *Judge, U. S. Court of Appeals, Washington, D. C.*

CLYDE B. VEDDER, *Department of Sociology and Anthropology, Northern Illinois University, DeKalb, Illinois.*

TO PROBATION AND PAROLE OFFICERS EVERYWHERE from whom we have learned a great deal, and to N. Jeane Hartman whose assistance in the preparation of the manuscript has been of considerable substance.

PREFACE

In order to effect a lasting change in probationers and parolees it is necessary to teach them self-discipline; control over them is not enough. We have to take the policeman from the offender's elbow and put him in his head.

Control is a restraining power, while discipline refers to training, education and instruction to act in accordance with the rules. To a great extent the behavior or conduct of probationers and parolees has been self-defeating. Not because they want to chastize themselves but because they are the products of their distortion of their life experiences. If they have not learned to control their behavior, then they must be taught to do so if they are to function effectively as law abiding citizens. Probation and parole officers are expected to do what the parents, the schools, and the individual's experiences have not done for him. The officers must re-educate youngsters and adults who are already pretty much molded by teaching them self-discipline in a relatively short period of time (i.e., the term of probation or parole).

As agents of authority it is difficult for the officer not to lean too heavily upon the power that is vested in him, and to control the offender. There are times when it is all the agent can do to hold the "lid on the Id," that is, to control the individual, to restrain the offender so that he will not harm himself or others. But control and restraint are not sufficient to effect lasting change. When the individual needs to be restrained, perhaps he should be placed in a closed institution where the treatment people can work with him. Most offenders represent no grave threat to themselves or to others.

Control and restraint produce anxiety, an uneasiness about the future. In socializing the individual he must be restrained initially (as in the case of a child) because he does not know what the consequences of his behavior will be; and as he grows he must still be controlled because he does not attach the same meanings to the consequences of his behavior as we do. The mature individual is concerned with the consequences of his behavior both for himself and for others, as well as the meanings attached by the dominant culture to the behavior at issue. He is able to keep himself in line with the expectations or rules imposed on him. In fact, a measure of maturity is this ability to function effectively in the environment which confronts us.

Given sufficient pressure the most mature of us will lose our self-control, even those of us who see ourselves as the very model of self-discipline. This, however, does not mean that all is lost, because for the larger part the mature individual can exercise self-discipline in respect to the more important parts of his life and is able to consummate his plans for the future while coping with the present.

Most of the probationers and parolees with whom we have contact come from rather deprived economic backgrounds. They have fashioned a way of life for themselves in keeping with the tools that our socio-economic structure has allowed them. Their experiences have fashioned them into fatalists who believe that "Whatever will be, will be," and "Get while the getting's good." It is fine to plan for the future when the present is taken care of, and the past has demonstrated that, if we plan, the reward will be greater due to our ability to control our behavior. But, when the past has demonstrated that "He who hesitates is lost," and the present produces nothing but anxiety over the future, the basis for action takes on the appearance of uncontrolled, random participation which could be explained as a form of short-run hedonism.

Most probationers and parolees have no logical reason to try to meet the probation or parole officers' expectations for them. Initially their reaction to the agents of authority will be anxiety or fear, or, in the case of the more "sophisticated" and/or experienced offenders, an attitude of total indifference may prevail. Only after the agent has demonstrated that he attaches worth and dignity to the client, and that he is willing to allow the client the right to self-determination (some self-esteem), will it be possible for the offender to learn self-discipline through a meaningful relationship. The offender will be concerned about the agent's expectations for him, because the relationship is one of mutual trust and respect. The offender will gain satisfaction for himself in the exercise of self-discipline, through the sanctions the officer places on his acceptable behavior. He will find dignity and worth within himself as a person who is able to control his behavior.

Expectations must be realistic and in keeping with the individual's ability to handle life situations. Conditions of probation and parole find some justification indirectly in the inability of the untrained individual to stay away from activities which are highly associated with law violation. It is not sufficient to hand the client a list of conditions of probation or parole. For the conditions to be meaningful for the individual, interpretation is required. Probation and parole regulations or conditions may often be characterized as redundant, complex, inconsistent, irrelevant and confused by legal jargon. The contradiction of probation and parole is the expectation that an offender can behave in a completely normal way while he is enmeshed in abnormal requirements.

The content of this book was selected for practitioners and other students of probation, parole and correction. It is our hope that the book will bring to the reader both greater depth and breadth of understanding relevant to probation and parole as meaningful adjuncts to the total correctional process. The writers believe that a more extensive and realistic use of probation and parole are central to the successful handling of offenders and, in turn, a partial solution to the total problem of crime.

B.A.K.
C.B.V.

CONTENTS

Page

Contributors v

Preface ix

PART I
PROBATION

Chapter

1. THE LEGAL ORIGINS OF PROBATION—*United Nations* 3
2. THE DEVELOPMENT OF PROBATION IN THE UNITED STATES—
   United Nations 14
3. THE PRESENTENCE INVESTIGATION—*Edmond Fitzgerald* 28
4. INTERVIEWING CANDIDATES FOR PROBATION—*Chester H. Bartoo* 53
5. PRISON OR PROBATION—WHICH AND WHY?—*Alfred Murrah* .. 62
6. PROBATIONARY SUPERVISION: CONTENTS, PERSONNEL AND
   ORGANIZATION—*United Nations* 69
7. PROBATION ADDENDUM—*Clyde B. Vedder and Barbara A. Kay* 88

PART II
PAROLE

8. PRINCIPLES OF PAROLE—*United Nations* 93
9. PRINCIPLES OF AFTER-CARE—*United Nations* 107
10. A SUMMARY OF PAROLE RULES—*Nat R. Arluke* 115
11. PAROLE PREDICTION—*Peter P. Lejins* 125
12. SOME DANGERS IN PAROLE PREDICTION—*Ralph W. England, Jr.* 132
13. CURRENT THINKING ON PAROLE PREDICTION TABLES—*Victor H.
    Evjen* 139
14. IT'S TIME TO START COUNTING—*J. Douglas Grant* 178
15. PAROLE ADDENDUM—*Barbara A. Kay and Clyde B. Vedder* ... 185

Bibliography 190

Probation and Parole

PART I

PROBATION

1

THE LEGAL ORIGINS OF PROBATION*

T HE ORIGIN, DEVELOPMENT and fate of specific methods for the treatment of offenders can be properly understood only against the wider background of contemporary cultural, social and economic forces. In so far as crime is defined as socially undesirable behavior subject to legal sanctions, the primary and constant object of criminal policy is the elimination or reduction of crime. The use or avoidance of specific methods, however, has varied very widely in both time and space, and these variations have tended to correspond with variations in social and political structure, in levels of knowledge, and in cultural values.[1]

Probation is an essentially modern method for the treatment of offenders and as such, it is rooted in the broader social and cultural trends of the modern era. In the history of criminal policy, the development of probation and related measures constitutes an integral part of the more general movement away from the traditional punitive and repressive approach, and towards the substitution of humanitarian and utilitarian considerations for considerations of general deterrence and retribution. This modern trend

---

*Probation and Related Measures. New York, United Nations, Department of Social Affairs, E/CN/.5/230, 1951, pp.15–26.

[1]Cf. Thorsten Sellin, "Foreword." to George Rusche and Otto Kirchheimer *Punishment and Social Structure* (1939), p. vi: "Fundamentally .... the aim of all punishment is the protection of those social values which the dominant social group of a State regard as good for 'society'....The means to secure the protection of 'society' have varied greatly because the law-enforcing powers of different societies have chosen those means which they believed to be at a given time most likely to secure obedience to their law. These beliefs are in turn dependent on tradition, the level of knowledge, and the nature of social economic institutions and conditions. The sanguinary punishment and tortures of old are no evidence of bloodthirstiness or sadism on the part of those who used them. They rather testify to the fact that those who designed them could conceive of no better, that is, more efficient, way of securing protection for the social values which they treasured. The character of punishments, then, is inextricably associated with and dependent on the cultural values of the State that employs them."

3

coincides with attempts to prevent crime by the improvement of social conditions and by the development of social services. It is characterized, furthermore, by the recognition of the social rehabilitation of the individual offender as a main object of criminal policy, and the rational selection and development of effective means to this end.

The origin of probation was not the result of a deliberate creative, legislative or judicial act, but rather the result of gradual growth, and almost unconscious modification of existing legal practices.

THE ORIGINS OF PROBATION AND ENGLISH COMMON LAW

Several attempts have been made to trace back the legal origins of probation to mediaeval and early modern European law. The precedents found in this period of legal history, however, generally relate to the suspension of punishment subject to good behavior rather than to probation as such, that is, a *combination* of the conditional suspension of punishment and the personal supervision of the released offender during a trial period. There can be little doubt that there has not been any continuous process of historical development linking early Continental instances of the use of the conditional suspension of punishment with contemporary probation. Probation as it is known today has been derived from the practical extension of the English common law, and an analysis of the legal origins of probation must therefore be principally concerned with England and America.

In England and the United States of America probation developed out of various methods for the conditional suspension of punishment. Generally speaking, the court practices in question were inaugurated, or adopted from previously existing practices, as attempts to avoid the mechanical application of the harsh and cruel precepts of a rigorous, repressive criminal law. Among these Anglo-American judicial expedients which have been mentioned as direct precursors of probation, are the so-called benefit of clergy, the judicial reprieve, the release of an offender on his own recognizance, provisional release on bail, the provisional "filing" of a case, and other legal devices for the suspension of either the imposition or the execution of sentence, with a view to a full understanding of the legal origins of probation, it is necessary to review briefly the nature of these practices.

The Benefit of Clergy

The so-called benefit of clergy was a special plea of devious origin by virtue of which certain categories of offenders could, after conviction, but before judgment, claim exemption from, or mitigation of, punishment. In practice is was primarily a device to avoid capital punishment. The importance of this plea in the criminal proceedings of the eighteenth and early nineteenth century is beyond any doubt: "According to the common practice in England of working out modern improvements through antiquated forms, this exemption was made the means of modifying the severity of the criminal law." It is, however, extremely doubtful whether this device had any direct influence on the later development of the suspension of sentence or of any other immediate precursor of probation.

The Judicial Reprieve

The judicial reprieve was a temporary suspension by the court of either the imposition or the execution of a sentence. It was used for specific purposes such as to permit a convicted person to apply for a pardon, or under circumstances such as where the judge was not satisfied with the verdict or where the evidence was suspicious. Although this measure involved only a temporary stay of imposition or execution of sentence, it did lead, in some cases, to an abandonment of prosecution. It does not appear, however, that in England this device "was ever extended to embrace what is now termed an indefinite suspension of sentence, particularly in cases which presented no peculiar reasons, arising out of the lack of or limitations on procedure, for withholding execution of sentence." On the other hand, "there is, no doubt, more than a modicum of good reason in tracing the later pretensions of American courts to a power of indefinite suspension of sentence back to this early practice of reprieve in English courts."

The Recognizance

The recognizance is a legal device deeply embedded in English law. It originated as a measure of preventive justice, and as such it "consists in obliging those persons, whom there is a probable ground to suspect of future misbehavior, to stipulate with and to give full assurance to the public, that such offence as is apprehended shall not happen . . . ." This "assurance to the public" is given by entering into a recognizance or bond (with or without sureties) creating a debt to the State which becomes enforceable, however, only when the specified conditions are not observed. The recognizance is entered into for a specified period of time.

At an early date the use of the principle of the recognizance (or binding-over) was also extended to actual offenders arraigned before the criminal courts. The device came to be used both to ensure the appearance of an offender before the court at a future date when called upon, and as a disposition (or part thereof) in the case of convicted offenders. With the passing of time, the recognizance came to be used almost exclusively with reference to criminal proceedings rather than as a measure of preventive justice. It should be noted, however, that the recognizance, when used in connection with persons arraigned before criminal courts, does not lose its character as a measure of preventive justice but is actually designed to ensure the future law behavior of the offender or, as Blackstone said, "must be understood rather as a caution against the repetition of the offence, than [as] any immediate pain or punishment."

For centuries the courts of England on occasion bound over and released minor offenders on their own recognizance, *with or without sureties*. Similarly, instances of this practice can be found in the records of the American colonies. During the first half of the nineteenth century this device was adopted with increasing frequency particularly in the case of youthful and petty offenders, the imprisonment of whom did not appear to be warranted. The practice seems to have been common in New England (particularly Massachusetts) at the time, and was to be found also in other jurisdictions of the United States of America.

The device of binding-over was used extensively and imaginatively by Judge Peter Oxenbridge Thacher during his term of office (1823-1843) in the Municipal Court of Boston, and the practices developed by him were of particular significance in the later development of probation in Massachusetts. The earliest recorded case in this connection is the case of *Commonwealth* vs. *Chase* (1830). In Judge Thacher's opinion we find in this case a clear statement of the nature of the practice of binding-over as employed by him:

> "The indictment against Jerusha Chase was found at the January term of this court, 1830. She pleaded guilty to the same, and sentence would have been pronounced at that time, but upon the application of her friends, and with the consent of the attorney of the commonwealth, she was permitted, upon her recognizance for her appearance in this court whenever she should be called for, to go at large. It has sometimes been practised in this court, in cases of peculiar interest, and in the hope that the party would avoid the commission of any offense afterwards, to discharge him on a recognizance of this description. The effect is, that no sentence will ever be pronounced against him, if he shall behave himself well afterwards, and avoid any further violation of the law...."

In 1836, the State of Massachusetts, as part of a general revision of its statutory law, gave legislative recognition to the practice of release upon recognizance, *with sureties,* at any stage of the proceedings, in so far as it applied to petty offenders in the lower courts. In the report of the commissioners charged with the revision of the statutory law of the State, the commissioners formulated the theoretical basis of this alteration in the law relating to the punishment of petty offenders, as follows:

> "This alteration consists in the discretionary power proposed to be given to the courts and magistrates, before whom this class of offenders may be brought, to discharge them, if they have any friends who will give satisfactory security for their future good behavior, for a reasonable time. When such sureties can be obtained, it can hardly fail to operate as a powerful check upon the conduct of the party, who is thus put upon his good behavior. And if his character and habits are such that no one will consent to be sponsor for him, it must forcibly impress on his mind the value of a good character, while it deprives him of all ground of just complaint of the severity of the law, or the magistrate."

It is significant to compare this formulation of the theory underlying the use of release on recognizance, with a British formulation of the second half of the nineteenth century. In a book published in 1877, Edward William Cox, Recorder of Portsmouth, specifically described the release of offenders on their own recognizance, with sureties, as a "substitute for punishment," and he noted that, while the conduct of the released offenders was proper, no further action was taken. In particular, he was strongly motivated by the desire to avoid the demoralizing and contaminating influence of short terms of imprisonment, especially in the case of first and juvenile offenders. As for the *rationale* of the use of the recognizances, with sureties, he says, "The suspension only of the judgment, the knowledge that if he [the offender] offends he may yet be punished —the hold which his bail thus has upon him, to a great extent guarantee that if there is in him an inclination to redeem himself he will return to a life of honesty."

Provisional Release on Bail

It has been noted in the preceding paragraphs that the device of releasing an offender on his own recognizance (binding-over) may be used *with or without sureties*. Conversely, the device of sureties (or bail) may be employed either with or without simultaneously binding over the defendant on his own recognizance. The significance of the device of sureties, when combined with the recognizance, as a precursor of probation, has already been discussed; it remains to be pointed out, however, that both in England and in the United States of America the device of bail as such (that is, when not used in conjunction with the recognizance) has similarly been of major historical significance in the evolution of probation, namely, as a device for the provisional suspension of punishment in relation to rudimentary probation practices.

Binding-over, Bail and the Origins of Probation

It has been noted above, that the recognizance is essentially a preventive rather than a punitive measure of dealing with actual or potential offenders. In the early nineteenth century the increased use of this device was motivated, no doubt, to a considerable extent by considerations of mercy and in this respect the device was one of the measures employed to reduce the hardships involved in the mechanical application of a rigorous criminal law. The rehabilitative object of the measure—i.e., the prevention of crime by the restoration of the offender as a law-abiding member of society—was, however, always present. Nevertheless, during this era the device came to be applied with an increasing realization of its rehabilitative potentialities, and came to be accompanied by increasingly effective safeguards and aids in the form of the personal supervision of, and assistance to, the released offender during the trial period. It should further be noted that the recognizance has always contained the germs of supervision—it involves the conditional suspension of punishment, and some vigilance is required to ascertain whether the conditions concerned are being complied with.

It is clear that the provisional release of offenders in the charge of sureties similarly contained the germs of probationary supervision (irrespective of whether this device was combined with the recognizance or not). In view of their financial interest in the conduct of the provisionally released offender, sureties are bound to try to ensure the good behavior of the offender through personal supervision, assistance or influence. The deliberate use, by the courts, of the salutory influence of sureties on offenders released conditionally, either on their own recognizance or on bail, indeed seems to have been in a very real sense the first, rudimentary stage in the development of probation.

The Provisional "Filing" of Cases

The practice of provisionally "filing" a case seems to have been peculiar to Massachusetts. This device consisted of the suspension of the imposition of sentence when, "after verdict of guilty in a criminal case .... the Court is satisfied that, by reason of extenuating circumstances, or of the pendency of a question of law in a like case before a higher court, or other sufficient reason, public justice does not require an immediate sentence...." The use of this procedure was subject to the consent of the defendant and of the prosecuting attorney, and the suspension was made subject to such conditions as the court in its discretion might impose. The order that a case be laid on file was not equivalent to a final judgment, but left it within the power of the court to take action on the case at any time, upon motion of either party.

CONCLUSION: THE SUSPENSION OF SENTENCE
AT COMMON LAW

By way of summary, it may be noted that there existed, during the nineteenth century and earlier, several legal devices which enabled the English and the American courts to suspend either the imposition of sentence (recognizance to keep the peace or to be of good behavior and to appear for judgment when called upon, provisional release on bail, the provisional "filing of a case," and the judicial reprieve) or the execution of sentence (also the judicial reprieve). That these devices existed, and allowed *at least* for the *temporary* suspension of sentence for *specific purposes,* is beyond any doubt. The question whether the English and American courts possess, at common law, an inherent power to suspend sentence *indefinitely* is, however, more problematic.

In analysing the question of an inherent judicial power to suspend sentence *indefinitely,* it is necessary to distinguish clearly between the use of the special devices of the recognizance and bail, on the one hand, and other devices used for the provisional suspension of punishment, on the other hand. Prior to statutory provisions to this effect, the courts both in England and in the United States of America *did,* in fact, engage in the suspension of the imposition of sentence when releasing offenders on their own recognizances, and took no further action with regard to the infliction of punishment if the condition of good behavior was complied with. Similarly, this procedure was followed, prior to statutory authorization, in at least two of the other countries of the British Commonwealth, viz., New Zealand and Canada. Both in England and in certain jurisdictions of the United States of America (notably Massachusetts), the conditional suspension of the imposition of sentence, with the ultimate release of the offender from all punishment in case of good behavior, was practised (without statutory authorization) also in relation to the provisional release of offenders on bail.

For all practical purposes it may be said that—beyond the relatively circumscribed practice of suspending the imposition of a sentence by means of releasing an offender on a recognizance and-/or bail—the English courts *did not* assume the existence of an inherent common law power to suspend sentence indefinitely. In the United States of America, however, a variety of practices developed, with a tendency to extend the suspension of sentence beyond the employment of the recognizance and/or bail. In particular, this involved the suspension of the imposition or of the execution of sentence on the basis of the common law precedent of the judicial reprieve. With the increasing use of the conditional suspension of punishment, with or without some sort of probationary supervision, courts in different jurisdictions adopted contradictory points of view on the question of the existence, at common law, of an inherent judicial power of indefinite suspension of sentence. While some held that the courts had such a power, others rejected this view arguing either that the conditions justifying the recognition of such a power in England did not obtain in the United States, or that the indefinite suspension of sentence by the court constituted an encroachment on the executive prerogative of pardon and reprieve, and thus infringes upon the doctrine of the separation of powers.

The United States Supreme Court finally expressed itself on the issue in question in the so-called *Killits case*. In his opinion in this case, the late Chief Justice White decided that English common law did not give the Federal courts the power to suspend sentence indefinitely:

> "It is true that, owing to the want of power in common law courts to grant new trials and to the absence of a right to review convictions in a higher court, it is we think, to be conceded: (a) that both suspensions of sentence and suspensions of the enforcement of sentence, temporary in character, were often resorted to on grounds of error or miscarriage of justice which under our system would be corrected either by new trials or by the exercise of the power to review; (b) that not infrequently, where the suspension either of the imposition of a sentence or of its execution was made for the purpose of enabling a pardon to be sought or bestowed, by a failure to further proceed in the criminal cause in the future, although no pardon had been sought or obtained, the punishment fixed by law was escaped. But neither of these conditions serves to convert the mere exercise of a judicial discretion to temporarily suspend for the accomplishment of a purpose contemplated by law into

the existence of an arbitrary judicial power to permanently refuse to enforce the law."

With reference to the decision in the Killits case, the *Attorney
General's Survey* concludes as follows:

"For practical purposes it may be said that this decision
served to explode the erroneous belief that had grown up in
some States. . . . It may be concluded, therefore, that there is no
historical warrant in the English common law for the claim that
American courts have an inherent power to suspend sentence
indefinitely. Where this power has been asserted, it has been
based on a misconception of English authorities or recognized
because it tempered the criminal law with mercy and had grown
as a local practice."

It should be noted that Court's decision in the Killits case did
not seek to invalidate the practice of releasing offenders on their
own recognizances but referred to "the fact that common law
courts possessed the power by recognizances to secure good behavior, that is, to enforce the law. . . ." This fact did not, however,
afford support for "the proposition that those courts possessed the
arbitrary discretion to permanently decline to enforce the law."

From the point of view of the development of probation as a
distinct method for the treatment of offenders, the extent to which
the judicial devices in which it had its historical origins, were, in
fact, extra-legal and not warranted by the English common law,
is of small significance. The important point is that these devices
developed, and could in fact only develop, in a system of common
law jurisdiction which is flexible enough to allow for the gradual
adjustment of existing practices to new needs and new objectives.
In England this process of adjustment was more conservative and
it is probable that the courts stayed within their common law
powers; in any case, the legality of the devices used for the conditional suspension of punishment, in relation to early pre-statutory
probation practices, was never challenged in England, in Canada or
in New Zealand. In the United States of America, the courts over-
stepped their common law powers, and the resulting diversity and
confusion of principles and authorities necessitated the authoritative revision of the legal bases of the practices that have developed.

Nevertheless, the definitive explosion of the doctrine of an inherent judicial power to suspend sentence indefinitely came when probation was already a well established part of the administration of criminal justice, and when public opinion had already been fully prepared for this new method for the treatment of offenders. Consequently, the final rejection by the Supreme Court of the doctrine of a common law judicial power of indefinite suspension of sentence actually served as a stimulus for the enactment of statutes expressly authorizing the suspension of sentence and probation.

2

THE DEVELOPMENT OF PROBATION IN THE UNITED STATES*

MASSACHUSETTS

THE STATE OF MASSACHUSETTS shares with England the honour of having given the probation system to the world. During the first half of the nineteenth century, Massachusetts judges sought diligently and in a variety of ways to render the administration of justice more humane, and a favourable judicial climate was thus established for the development of rudimentary "probation" practices.

The first bold step taken beyond the initial rudimentary probation practices (consisting of release on recognizances with sureties) was taken in Boston in 1841. On a day in August of that year a local cobbler, John Augustus, attended the police court in that city, and decided to stand bail for a man charged with being a common drunkard. The court permitted this, and the defendant was ordered to appear for sentence in three weeks, at which time the defendant was brought back showing convincing signs of reform. Instead of the usual penalty—imprisonment in the House of Correction—the judge imposed a nominal fine of one cent and ordered the defendant to pay costs.

Encouraged by his first experience, Augustus proceeded to stand bail for more offenders, and to undertake the task of supervising and guiding their behavior during the period pending judgment. All the early cases handled by him were adult males charged with common drunkenness, but he gradually extended the scope of his activities to include women (at first also common drunkards) and children, and ultimately persons charged with a wide variety of offences. He also extended his activity to include work in the municipal court. Subsequently Augustus continued his labours for eighteen years until his death in 1859. During this period he

*Probation and Related Measures, New York, United Nations, Department of Social Affairs, E/CN/.5/230, 1951, pp.29–42.

14

"bailed on probation" almost 2,000 persons and achieved a very high proportion of successes.

During this period of his activities in the courts of Boston, John Augustus developed several of the features that later became characteristic of the probation system.

As regards the selection of probationers, he confined his efforts "mainly to those who were indicted for their first offence, and whose hearts were not wholly depraved, but gave promise of better things ...." He did not assume the responsibility for an offender "merely at the solicitation of the unfortunate, or without due investigation into the merits of their cases and a scrupulous examination into the history and character of each individual." "Great care was observed.... to ascertain whether the prisoners were promising subjects for probation, and to this end it was necessary to take into consideration the previous character of the person, his age and the influences by which he would in future be likely to be surrounded, and although these points were rigidly adhered to, still they were the circumstances which usually determined my action."

When Augustus undertook the responsibility for offenders, he agreed to "note their general conduct," and to "see that they were sent to school or supplied with some honest employment." In addition, he very often provided, or arranged for, accommodation.

He agreed also to make an impartial report to the court, whenever required to. In addition he maintained a careful register of all cases handled.

After the death of John Augustus, his work was continued by Rufus R. Cook, Chaplain to the county gaol and representative of the Boston Children's Aid Society, and other less well-known pioneer "probation officers" whose work was largely voluntary. These men "seem to have carried out the essential features of probation—investigation of defendant before release, the regular reports and home visits ... However, their work was of the 'rescue' sort.... It is evident that the investigations were necessarily meagre, that probation periods were very short (only a few weeks at the start), and that records, plans of treatment and close supervision were not much in evidence."

By a law of 1869, the State of Massachusetts provided for the appointment of a state agent of the Board of State Charities to investigate cases of children tried before the courts, to attend such trials and to receive children for placement if the court so ordered. The state agents appointed under this new measure (with the assistance of voluntary organizations) exercised supervision over the behavior of deliquent children placed on probation under the existing common law practice.

Probation came to be regulated by statute for the first time in 1878, when Massachusetts passed a law providing for the appointment of a paid probation officer for the courts of criminal jurisdiction in the city of Boston. It is of no mean significance that this pioneer statute on probation specifically contrasts probation with punishment by directing that "such persons as may reasonably be expected to be reformed without punishment" should be selected to be put on probation. Of equal significance is the fact that the statute does not restrict the application of probation to any particular class of offenders (first offenders, young offenders, etc.) or to any particular class of offences, but postulates the likelihood of the individual offender's being reformed without punishment, as the only criterion for the selection of offenders to be released on probation.

The Massachusetts statute of 1878 was designed to deal with the appointment and duties of a probation officer rather than with the legal issues involved in probation. It provided for the annual appointment, by the Mayor of Boston, of a "suitable person" either from the ranks of the police force of the city or "from the citizens at large." The incumbent of the position was to be "under the general control" of the chief of police of the city.

The statute prescribed the duties of the probation officer as including court attendance, the investigation of the cases of persons charged with or convicted of crimes or misdemeanours, the making of recommendations to the courts with regard to the advisability of using probation, the submission of periodical reports to the chief of police, visiting probationers, and the rendering of "such assistance and encouragement [to probationers] as will tend to prevent their again offending."

The statute further gave to the probation officer the power to re-arrest a probationer, without further warrant but with the approval of the chief of police; in such a case the court might "proceed to sentence or make such other disposition of the case as may be authorized by law."

In accordance with the provisions of the statute of 1878, the Mayor of Boston appointed Captain E. H. Savage, formerly Chief of Police, as first statutory probation officer. Generally speaking, the previously existing common law practice of probation remained unaltered, the only significant innovation being the official nature of the new arrangements for the exercise of probationary supervision. The practice of probation under this new arrangement is described as follows, in contemporary records:

"[The probation officer] obtains information from the police and in other ways regarding those who have been arrested, and when their cases are called for trial, he takes on probation by authority of the courts those who may reasonably be expected to reform without punishment.

"The term of probation ranges from three months to one year, under such conditions as seen best suited to the case. The officer becomes bondsman in a certain sum for the faithful performance of these conditions and for the prisoner's appearance at court from time to time until the case is finally disposed of. The time of continuance for appearance usually ranges from six to twelve weeks."

The correctional authorities in Massachusetts soon showed that they were aware of the importance of the new arrangements provided for by the statute of 1878. In their annual report published in 1880, the Prison Commissioners made reference to the "very important experiment" that was being tried in the city of Boston, and recommended that legislative provision be made for the extension of the system to other cities.

By a statute of 1880 the right to appoint probation officers was extended to all cities and towns in Massachusetts. In contrast with the statute of 1878 relating to Boston, the statute of 1880 was merely permissive and only a few towns or cities in the state exercised the option of appointing probation officers. Probation was established on a state-wide basis in Massachusetts in 1891, when an act was passed transferring the power of appointment of probation officers from the municipal authorities to the courts, and making such appointment mandatory instead of permissive. Each police district and each municipal court was required to appoint a probation officer, and the probation system was thereby firmly established throughout the lower courts of the state. It was extended to the superior courts by an act of 1898 which authorized the latter to appoint their own probation officers.

It should be noted that the Massachusetts statutes of 1878 to 1898 were designed to supplement, not supplant, the existing common law system of probation. The essential legal features of the common law system—the suspension of the imposition of sentence, "bailing on probation," and the return of the probationer to the court, to be discharged or disposed of otherwise, at the end of the probation period—were taken for granted. The statutes in question dealt primarily with the appointment, remuneration, control and duties of probation officers, and thus enabled the courts to use probation more freely and more effectively. In fact, the introduction of statutory provisions in relation to probation should be seen as an integral part of a continuous process of growth and development, applying both to the probation system in Massachusetts as such and to its acceptance by public opinion. Only this circumstance made it possible for the first probation statute in the world to be passed practically without public discussion or controversy.

THE SPREAD OF PROBATION—THE FIRST PHASE

Other states were slow in following the example of Massachusetts with regard to the adoption of probation. The appointment of probation officers had, in fact, been made mandatory in all the lower courts of Massachusetts before the subject was first dealt with in the statute law of any other state. Towards the end of the nineteenth century, however, significant developments in this connection began to take place in other states. At the close of the century six more states had made statutory provision for probation: Missouri (1897) ; Vermont (1898) ; Illinois, Minnesota and Rhode Island (1899) ; and New Jersey (1900).

Some of these early statutes introduced several significant innovations. Thus, Illinois and Minnesota made provision for juvenile probation only, while Rhode Island introduced restrictions with regard to the scope of the application of probation by excluding offenders convicted of specific serious offences. Missouri and Minnesota introduced the suspension of the *execution* of sentence instead of the suspension of the imposition of sentence. Vermont was the first state to adopt a county plan for the organization of probation—the act required the appointment of a probation officer by the county judge in each county of the state, each officer being assigned to all the courts in his county. Rhode Island, on the other hand, introduced a state-wide and state-controlled probation system, and was the first state to do so. In the meantime, probation was being developed also in a few other states (particularly in New York and Maryland) without authorizing legislation or with statutory provision for the suspension of sentence only.

THE JUVENILE COURT MOVEMENT AND THE SPREAD OF PROBATION

The development of probation in the United States of America after the beginning of the twentieth century is closely related to the juvenile court movement. In fact, it was "under the pressure of the juvenile court movement" that probation "was transformed from a local institution applied in different forms in a few states, into a national institution recognized by the legislation of all the states and territories, as well as by federal legislation. . . .

Separate provision for juvenile probation was first made in Minnesota by an act of 1899; this statute, however, merely limited the application of probation to juveniles and did not introduce any new instrumentality for the treatment of juvenile offenders. Later in the same year (1899), however, Illinois enacted a first juvenile court law, and initiated a powerful new movement in the field of criminal policy.

The Illinois statute of 1899 established a special juvenile court for Chicago (Cook County), and gave this court jurisdiction over all juvenile offenders up to the age of sixteen years. As an alternative to institutional treatment, the statute provides for the committal of a child "to the care and guardianship of a probation officer duly appointed by the court", such care and guardianship to be exercised while the child remains in his own home or while the child is placed or boarded out in a more suitable family home. The statute provides for the appointment of probation officers by the court, but specifically excludes their compensation from the public treasury, thus making the operation of the act dependent on the services of voluntary welfare organizations and individual volunteers. The duties of probation officers are defined in general accordance with the pattern established in Massachusetts legislation— "it shall be the duty of the said probation officer to make such investigation as may be required by the court, to be present in court in order to represent the interest of the child when the case is heard; to furnish to the court such information and assistance as the judge may require; and to take such charge of any child before and after trial as may be directed by the court. . . . "

The essential principles of the juvenile court are: (*a*) the acceptance of protection and guidance, instead of punishment, as the objectives of the treatment of juvenile offenders, and (*b*) the adoption of a flexible, individually adjusted plan of treatment for each offender. As a method of treatment, probation is one of the indispensable instruments of the juvenile court, and it is not surprising, therefore, that the rapid spread of the juvenile court throughout the country of its origin, and throughout the world, has constituted a tremendous force in the further development of probation.

THE SPREAD OF PROBATION SINCE 1900

In the United States of America, state legislative provision for probation spread rapidly between 1900 and 1915 and more slowly since 1915. The states with the most predominantly urban populations developed probation first and it spread gradually to the more rural states.

The introduction of probation in the different states generally tended to follow either the older pattern of probation as a method applicable by the criminal courts in general (the Masachusetts system), or the newer pattern of juvenile probation as an integral part of the juvenile court (the system initiated by Illinois). It should be noted that, as a variation on the first pattern, the application of probation by the criminal courts was in some cases limited to juveniles and, in such cases, the introduction of juvenile probation was not accompained by the establishment of juvenile courts. Finally, another minor trend, initiated by Colorado in 1903, originated as an outgrowth of, and supplement to, the juvenile court movement, and involved the creation of a limited form of adult probation, namely, probation applicable to parents and other persons responsible for or contributing to the delinquency of children.

Although general and adult probation represents the older pattern of probation legislation, probation was far more generally introduced for the first time as an integral part of the juvenile court. Thirty of the forty-eight states first introduced probation in juvenile court laws; eleven states first introduced probation in the criminal courts; four states and the District of Columbia first introduced probation as a criminal court measure limited to juveniles; and the remaining three states simultaneously introduced adult probation and juvenile courts (with provision for juvenile probation) . The years of the first enactment of probation and juvenile court laws in the United states of America are presented in Table 1.

Subsequent to the first enactment either of a probation law or of a juvenile court law, practically all the states tended to supplement the one with the other, thus completing the structure of this particular arm of modern systems of the administration of criminal justice. In the case of states that first made provision for general or adult probation, or for juvenile probation, the enactment of juvenile court laws generally followed without any considerable time lag, and by 1912 almost all the states in this category had enacted juvenile court laws. In the case of states that introduced probation through juvenile court laws, however, the extension of the application of probation to adults and to the general criminal courts in many cases followed only after a very considerable time lag. In fact, this time lag exceeded twenty-five years in fifteen of the thirty states in this category.

By 1910, thirty-five states and the District of Columbia had

Table 1

YEARS OF FIRST ENACTMENT OF PROBATION AND JUVENILE COURT LAWS
IN THE UNITED STATES OF AMERICA[a]

State or Territory (or other Delimitation of Jurisdiction)	General or Adult Probation Law[b]	Juvenile Probation Only[c]	Juvenile Court Law
Alabama	1939[d]	—	1907
Arizona	1913	—	1907
Arkansas	1937	—	1911
California	1903	—	1903
Colorado	1931[e]	—	1903[f]
Connecticut	1903	1903	1905
Delaware	1911	—	1911
Florida	—	—	1911
Dade, Duval and Hillsborough Counties	1939	—	—
State-wide	1940	—	—
Georgia	1907	—	1908
Atlanta	—	1904	—
Idaho	1915	—	1905
Illinois	1911	—	1899
Indiana	1907	—	1903
Iowa	1909	—	1904
Kansas	1907	1901	1905
Kentucky	1934	—	1906
Louisiana	1942	—	1906
Maine	1905	1905	—[g]
Maryland	1931[h]	—	1916
Baltimore	—	—	1902
Massachusetts	1891	1891	1906
Suffolk County	1878	1878	—
All cities and towns	1880	1880	—
Michigan	1903	1903	1905
Minnesota	1909	—	1905
Counties over 50,000	—	1899	—
Minors only	1903	—	—
Mississippi	—[i]	—	1916
Missouri	1897[j]	—	—
St. Louis City	—	1901	—
St. Louis and Jackson Counties	—	1903	—
Counties, 50,000 or more	—	—	1907
Smaller counties	—	—	1913
Montana	1913	—	1907
Nebraska	1909	—	1905
Nevada	—[i]	—	1909
New Hampshire	1937	—	1907
New Jersey	1900	1900	1903

Table 1 (continued)

State or Territory (or other Delimitation of Jurisdiction)	General or Adult Probation Law[b]	Juvenile Probation Only[c]	Juvenile Court Law
New Mexico	—[1]	—	1917
New York	1901	1903	1922
Buffalo	—	1901	—
New York City	—	—	1902
North Carolina	1937	—	1915
North Dakota	1909	1909	1911
Ohio	1908	—	1904
Cuyahoga County	—	—	1902
Oklahoma	—	—	1909
Oklahoma County	1939	—	—
Oregon	1931	—	1905
Pennsylvania	1909	—	1903[k]
Rhode Island	1899	1899	1909
South Carolina	1941	—	1912
South Dakota	—[1]	—	1909
Tennessee	1915	—	1905
Texas	1947	—	1907
Utah	1923	1903	1905
Vermont	1898	1898	1912
Virginia	1910[l]	—	1910
Washington	1921	—	1905
West Virginia	1927	—	1915
Wisconsin	1909	—	1901
Wyoming	1941	—	1945
District of Columbia	1910	1901	1906
Territory of Alaska	1925[m]	—	1913
Territory of Hawaii	1931	—	1905
Territory of Puerto Rico	1925[m]	—	1915
United States (Federal) Courts	1925	1925	—

[a]Based on Cosulich, *Adult Probation Laws of the United States*, 2nd edition (1940), pp. 12-15 *Attorney General's Survey*, Vol. II, p. 27; Tompkins, *Sources for the Study of the Administration of Criminal Justice* (1949), pp. 233-234; and National Probation [and Parole] Association *Yearbook*, 1941-1948. *Cf.* footnote[48] in the text.

[b]States having adult probation only in the juvenile courts—in cases of adults contributing to the delinquency or neglect of children—are not classified as having adult probation laws.

[c]This column is used only for states where juvenile probation was introduced by statute independent of and prior to the enactment of juvenile court legislation.

[d]An earlier act, passed in 1931, was declared unconstitutional in 1935.

[e]This act was preceded by the *Redemption of Offenders Act,* 1909, which introduced what was virtually an adult probation system.

adopted juvenile court laws, while statutory provision for adult probation had been made in twenty-one states and in the District of Columbia. By 1917, forty-six states (all but Maine and Wyoming) had enacted juvenile court laws, and the number having adult probation legislation had increased to twenty-seven in 1915. The further spread of adult probation was much slower: during the period 1916 to 1930 only three more states enacted such legislation, and probation was also introduced into Federal criminal legislation. The movement regained momentum in the nineteen-thirties during which period ten more states enacted adult probation legislation, bringing the total to forty. Subsequently the total has further increased to forty-four, leaving four states without statutory provision for adult probation.

SUSPENSION-OF-SENTENCE STATUTES

With the progressive enactment of probation statutes in most of the states, there also appeared a tendency to enact statutes authorizing the suspension of sentence. This tendency was related, in the first instance, to the fact that several higher courts, and particularly the United States Supreme Court in the Killits case, had invalidated the wide-spread belief in an inherent judicial power, at

---

[f]This act was preceded by the *School Offenders Act,* 1899, which provided for "truant officers" to deal with children between the ages of 8 and 14 years who were "habitual truants from school", or were 'incorrigible, vicious, or of immoral conduct," while their committal to children's homes was conditionally suspended. Under this law Judge Lindsey developed his famous juvenile court in Denver, using school truant officers as probation officers.

[g]Special procedure for dealing with juvenile offenders instituted in 1909.

[h]This act was preceded by a statute of 1894 under which probation was developed although the statute provided only for the suspension of sentence.

[j]Suspension-of-sentence statute only.

[i]The 1897 statute provided for so-called "bench parole"; an adult probation law proper was enacted in 1937.

[k]An earlier act of 1901 was declared unconstitutional.

[l]The 1910 statute was of limited application only in the case of adults (limited to persons charged with habitual intoxication, non-support of wife and children, vagrancy and idleness). An adult probation law of general application was enacted in 1918.

[m]The Federal *Probation Act.*

common law, to suspend sentence indefinitely. The continuance of the long-existing practice of suspending sentence—a practice which had developed under what was presumed to be common law authority—therefore required specific statutory authorization. This solution was, in fact, suggested by several courts in their decisions denying the existence of the common law power in question.

An additional factor which probably influenced legislatures to enact suspension-of-sentence statutes is to be found in the belief that such statutes constituted a step in the direction of the development of probation proper:

> "Many legislatures, aware of the worth of a probation system but timorous as yet of going all the way in adopting probation statutes, may have hoped that they could achieve the benefits of the Massachusetts system by half measures. Accordingly, statutes were passed in the belief that in authorizing courts to save defendants from the disgrace of incarceration in certain instances, some of the beneficial features of probation were being extended. . . . In fairness to the lawmakers who enacted these statutes, it should be borne in mind that in many instances they very probably entertained the hope and belief that their task was merely to remove certain restrictions under which the courts had labored and that in so doing they were providing a framework upon which the citizens and the courts of the State might work out, on their own initiative, a volunteer probation system along the same lines as the one which evolved in Massachusetts."

These sanguine hopes were unfortunately not realized in practice, and the enactment of suspension-of-sentence statutes in many cases was tantamount to the institution of "a practice of releasing convicted persons without sufficient investigation concerning their fitness for such treatment and without provision for any period of supervision."

In many cases supension-of-sentence statutes merely represented an intermediate step preceding the enactment of probation statutes proper. Up to the present, however, no such step beyond suspension-of-sentence statutes has been taken in the states of Mississippi, Nevada, New Mexico, Oklahoma (except in Oklahoma County) and South Dakota.

CONSTITUTIONAL OBSTACLES

In a few states constitutional obstacles were encountered in the enactment of probation legislation and, more commonly, of suspension-of-sentence legislation. The doctrine of the separation of powers, and the interpretation of the suspension-of-sentence as an encroachment on the executive prerogative of pardon, on occasion presented a formidable obstacle in this regard. Special amendments to the state constitutions of Texas and Alabama preceded the enactment of probation statutes in those states. Generally speaking, however, the constitutionality of probation statutes has only been questioned in a very few instances, and in most cases the courts have upheld the power of the legislature to enact such statutes.

CONCLUSION

The present résumé of the development of probation in the United States of America has been concerned primarily with the rise of probation in Massachusetts, its introduction into statute law, and the spread of probation legislation throughout the country. It was shown that the Massachusetts process of development was not duplicated anywhere else. The pioneer statutes of this state, together with the pioneer juvenile court legislation of Illinois, served as general models on which other states fashioned their probation legislation, and such legislation tended in the long run to embody provisions both for adult probation and for juvenile courts (with juvenile probation). It was pointed out, moreover, that innovations in the Massachusetts pattern were not limited to the introduction of probation in the juvenile court setting, but that various other internal variations in the probation system were already introduced by the half-a-dozen states that followed the lead of Massachusetts in enacting probation statutes before the close of the nineteenth century. This process of introducing internal variations into the system has continued to the present day, with the result that at present very considerable differences, as to *particular* aspects, obtain between legislative provisions as well as administrative practices with respect to probation in different states. Some of these internal variations in the probation system, as it exists in the United States of America, no doubt constitute limitations on the full and most constructive application of probation, and considerable regional and rural-urban inequalities exist in this respect. On the whole, however, it may be concluded that probation, in its essential elements, has become firmly established in the administration of criminal justice in the United States of America. The first phase—when "the battle was one for the extension of the system and the acceptance of the idea"—has passed, and the present-day concern is with the improvement of organization, administration and co-ordination; with the improvement of methods of probationary supervision and treatment; with the training of probation officers; and with the establishment and improvement of standards for the service in general.

3

THE PRESENTENCE INVESTIGATION*

O<small>N AN</small> A<small>PRIL NIGHT IN</small> 1947, <small>A BURGLAR</small> entered a bedroom window of a second floor apartment in the Brownsville section of Brooklyn. Asleep in the room was a fifteen-year-old girl. Her eleven-year-old brother slept in an adjoining room. Their parents were out for the evening.

From the facts as now known, it is safe to assume that the intruder's object was larceny, or at least there is no proof that he had anything else in mind. He was diverted from this purpose, however, when the girl awoke. He stifled her screams of alarm, but not before they had brought her little brother rushing to her room. The burglar beat the boy almost into insensibility, then resumed his onslaught on the moaning girl. She was dead and her attacker had vanished empty-handed into the night when neighbors responded to the boy's pleas for help several minutes later. The bedroom was a shambles—mute testimony of the terrific battle put up by the girl before her life was snuffed out.

This particular offender was not arrested until some two months after the crime and then only as a result of an intensive manhunt and some brilliant detective work. On arrest he was charged with first degree murder. He confessed readily and re-enacted the crime for the police. Notwithstanding the confession, the defendant was taken to trial since, in New York as in some other jurisdictions, pleas of guilty cannot be accepted in capital cases. He was defended spiritedly by three eminent attorneys assigned by the state. Their strategy was to attack the confession, which was the principal item of the prosecution's evidence, by contending that it had been obtained by police coercion, an argument in which the defendant himself now vigorously joined. Despite the efforts of the lawyers, the jury returned a verdict of murder, first degree, after a two-weeks' trial. The defense strategy was partially successful, however, in (presumably) influencing the jury to recommend that

*Edmond Fitzgerald: *National Probation and Parole Association Journal, 2:* 320–336, 1956.

the court exercise leniency in the disposition. This type of recommendation, permissible in felony murder cases (i.e., murders committed during the course of commission of a felony—in this case a burglary— but otherwise unpremeditated) , has the effect of enabling the trial judge to sentence to life imprisonment instead of to execution, as would be mandatory in the absence of such a recommendation from the jury.

Upon conviction, the defendant was immediately processed for presentence investigation by the court's probation department, as is customary. When he appeared for sentence a few weeks later, the court chose to ignore the jury's recommendation and sentenced him to the electric chair. In imposing the death penalty, the court adverted to the heinous nature of the crime, as disclosed by the trial testimony, and also remarked on some of the contents of the probation report.

The conviction and judgment were upheld upon appeal. The defense attorneys thereupon carried their case to the United States Supreme Court on constitutional grounds. Specifically, they singled out for attack two items from the probation report which the judge had mentioned in passing sentence and which were not otherwise "on the record." One was a reference to "some thirty prior burglaries" allegedly commited by the defendant at bar; the other was a fleeting comment on his "morbid sexuality" (the judge's own words) . Due process, the lawyers contended, would require that the accused be properly notified of these charges if they were to be entertained against him at any stage of the proceedings; that he be permitted to confront and cross-examine those making the allegations and to put them on their proof; and that he be given an opportunity for rebuttal.

AN EPOCH-MAKING CASE

The Supreme Court denied the appeal, upholding the conviction and the judgment of the trial court. The decision, now known in the legal annals as *New York* v. *Williams,* meant, among other things, that for the first time in its history of 100 years the probation movement had arrived at a point where its major operating instrument, the presentence investigation and report, earned and received validation "at the summit." The Supreme Court did much more than affirm the constitutional propriety of the document. It spelled out—more simply and more sensibly than any textbook or any propagandist had ever done—the philosophy and the ideals which animate, or should animate, the relationships of probation to the courts it serves on the one hand and the clients (defendants) it serves on the other. Of perhaps greater importance from the operational point of view, the decision put the stamp of constitutional approval on the methods and the objectives which give, or should give, probation its justification as an integral process in the even-handed administration of criminal justice in our complex modern society.

STATUTORY DEVELOPMENT

Probation, both in conception and development, is America's distinctive contribution to progressive penology. I would like to make a point of this phrase "distinctively American," because some of the textbooks go to great lengths to trace its origins back to British common law and to what Dean Roscoe Pound calls "the received ideals" of Continental legal systems. In this they are wrong. The development of probation has been entirely statutory, certainly so insofar as the system is an expression of *planned state policy*. Probation in America is characterized principally not by affinities with, but by deliberate divergences from, the common law and European precedents in general.

One of the interesting things to observe over the span of the century is the degree to which our entire philosophy of criminal law —and not merely that phase of it represented by probation—is moving farther and farther away from old-world antecedents as the years go on. In the older countries, when there still was some political and economic stability, the identifying hallmark of the legal philosophy could be described as reverence for precedent and for time-honored institutions and resistance to radical change. In England the historical record is one of a legal system slowly and cautiously—ever so slowly and ever so cautiously—adapting itself to the changing needs and talents of the people. It took them a long time, for example, to relax the lengthy syllabus of excessively punitive sanctions which were applied even to minor offenders up to comparatively recent times. The death penalty or mutilation was provided until well into the nineteenth century for some offenses that would today be considered trivial. It is typical of the British that the moderation of the penal statutes, when this finally came about, resulted from the slow momentum of unfolding history rather than from the initiative of Parliament or of any specific man or movement.

It is true that the momentum has been helped along here and there by the venalities of rulers (e.g., King John and Magna Charta) ; or by the disputations of philosophers (e.g., Bentham's *Principles of Morals and Legislation*) ; or by the barbs of satirists (e.g., Jonathan Swift's *Drapier's Letters* and its influence on the repeal of a whole series of penal laws aimed not so much at crime control as at suppression of civil liberties). But in the main the record shows that, for the Englishman, the pragmatic test sufficed: if his laws worked some-how and if they did not bother him personally, he was not interested in seeing how they worked and he was not disposed to tamper with them overmuch. And similarly on the Continent.

In America, by contrast, the tendency was—and is—not to regard tradition as necessarily sacred. We have never been interested in preserving the *status quo,* except to maintain our "inalienable rights" and our constitutional freedoms. This is perhaps inevitable in a polity which has grown as rapidly as ours has. The pace of economic expansion, of receding frontiers, of polyglot population increase, of proliferating technology, has made it difficult for governmental forms to keep abreast. It is not surprising, therefore, that legislative policy, in penal no less than in other spheres, has been determined more by the utilitarian needs of the growing community than by precedent or tradition. And probation is nothing if not utilitarian.

The generally accepted definition of probation, as applied to adult offenders at any rate, is about as follows: a form of disposition under which a court suspends either the sentence or execution of the judgment of sentence on selected offenders, releasing them conditionally on good behavior, under prescribed terms and rules and subject to the control, guidance, and assistance of the court as exercised through officers appointed to supervise them. The essence of the system is the conditional suspension of sentence *plus* supervision of all the activities of the defendant (probationer) for the period of the suspension. It was in America that the combination was first set in motion, by the judges of the Boston Municipal Court in cooperation with John Augustus. It was accomplished, in the beginning, not in any continuous process of historical development arising out of early British or Continental use of the conditional suspension, but rather in an ingenious departure from, or distortion of, the precedents.

For many years and in several jurisdictions in the United States, the courts proceeded on the theory that there was an inherent power at common law to suspend sentences on convicted criminals indefinitely. The fact is, however, that apart from a relatively circumscribed practice of invoking the procedures known as "benefit of clergy" and "judicial reprieve," the British courts had never assumed or claimed any such inherent power. In actuality, both benefit of clergy and judicial reprieve were little more than artifices to avoid imposition of full legal process; they were employed principally to delay or avert punishment in cases where the courts felt the prescribed penalty for the given offense to be either "out of order" or excessive for the particular individual convicted. In that sense, the devices were negative rather than positive. Both were used in the colonies for some years but were found to be of uneven or unsatisfactory application. They were later practically abandoned as the American courts began to confer upon themselves the right to make positive suspensions for fixed periods, by which is meant purposeful suspensions with the stated or implicit objective of regeneration and with definite or determinate time limits. They fell into complete disuse after probation emerged as an accepted legal system.

This acceptance of probation did not come about quietly or automatically. Throughout the later part of the nineteenth century and well into the twentieth, judges and lawyers had considerable difficulty in reconciling the system with the existing scheme of things, mainly because of the absence of established legal and procedural precedents. A number of appeals arose, for instance, in various states out of the question as to whether placements on probation represented a judicial invasion of the executive's pardoning prerogative under the "separation of powers" doctrine. The New York Court of Appeals, in ruling on an appeal from a suspension of sentence and grant of probation in 1894, upheld the trial court's action over the prosecutor's appeal but stated that its opinion "must not be understood as conferring any new power, because the power to suspend was inherent in all Superior Courts of criminal jurisdiction at common law." This decision was later discovered to be based largely on a misconstruction, if not indeed misquotation, of a famous passage in Lord Hale's *Pleas of the Crown* describing a practice which had grown up under British law. Chief Justice White, of the United States Supreme Court, commenting on the decision, referred to the misquotation from Lord Hale as "complete error," stating that in a diligent examination of *Pleas of the Crown* he found no passage containing the clauses cited by the New York Court of Appeals.

Chief Justice White thus demolished any lingering theory of common-law antecedents for probation. As a consequence, its further development had to be entirely statutory; in the past fifty years hundreds of enabling laws have been passed, providing for probation service of either statewide or local coverage.

One by-product of what might be called the "illegitimate" origins of probation is that while its philosophy and objectives have always met with ready acceptance, its methods have not, at any rate not to the same extent. Notwithstanding that broad definitions of rules and procedures have often been enunciated, legislatively and otherwise, their testing and refinement was a long, difficult, and not always completely understood experimental process. Not until the Supreme Court review of probation's policies and practices in the momentous Williams decision did these finally achieve constitutional acceptability, so to speak. The Williams case, then, is epochal in the sense that it became the agent through which the husky hundred-year-old probation infant was "legitimatized."

CAREFULLY CALCULATED RISKS

The core of the probation service is, of course, the catalogue of treatment services it provides for those offenders whom the courts consider *reasonable* (not necessarily synonymous with *safe*) risks to remain at large under supervision in the free community. This implies that selection for probationary release is based on careful calculation of the offender's strengths and weaknesses, both personal and social—on a finding that the positive factors in his total situation counterbalance the negative factors to a degree sufficient to warrant some expectation that he has, or can be helped to acquire, the capacity to repair the damage he had done to himself and the community and to handle himself in relation to others in such a manner as to secure whatever maximum of social and individual good might be attainable.

In the early history of the movement, the calculation of risk was often little better than a gamble, although in the less populous communities the offender's history and circumstances were often known personally to the judge, who could, therefore, assess risk satisfactorily enough without the formality of "presentence investigation" as we now understand the term. Such instances undoubtedly occur today,[1] but they are exceptional. If there ever was a time in which judges anywhere could be sure of really "knowing" any substantial number of the defendants who appeared before them, it has long since receded into the past.

Even in the early years, sentencing judges felt the need for more objective and dependable standards for selection of probationers than that afforded by *external* knowledge of the individual and his social milieu. In any case, this business of "knowing" people is a relative matter. Delinquents and criminals, as such, tend to be unknown even to their families and politer friends. Proper selection of eligible candidates for probation requires the identification and critical evaluation of those hidden urges and unconscious motivations, those quirks in personal and interpersonal attitudes, which, in a sense, make offenders "unknown" even to themselves. Out of these discoveries, which were helped along immeasurably by the contributions of the behavioral sciences, grew the small beginnings

---

[1] The Supreme Court gives a nod in this direction when it offers this incidental observation *in re* the due process question: "Of course, in the smaller communities sentencing judges, naturally, have in mind their knowledge of the personalities and backgrounds of convicted offenders."

of that disciplined exploration of the offender's past history and future possibilities that we now call "the presentence investigation."

PURPOSE OF THE INVESTIGATION

Originally intended as a guide to the court in estimating probation risks, the investigation soon came to have uses transcending this. Even before probation had been absorbed into the generic social work movement, the investigation report had come to be the repository for all biographical data needed not only for supervision in the free community but also for planning and executing rehabilitative programs for offenders committed to prisons and reformatories. Thus, the investigation (diagnostic) process, became as important as the rehabilitation (treatment) process. It is, in fact, of greater importance, since it is the bedrock of treatment. Quantitatively, it is now the most significant part of all probation work. This is true, at any rate, in most courts of higher criminal jurisdiction. The best available statistics show that in these courts, probably because of the very character of the offenses with which they deal, the ratio of probation placements to total dispositions is only 30 or 35 per cent. The vast majority of the remaining 65 to 70 per cent are prison commitments, not infrequently under mandatory statutes. Even for this residue, the investigation report has become an indispensable instrument in making imprisonment a constructive instead of a brutalizing experience. Accordingly, most progressive jurisdictions nowadays investigate *all* convicted offenders.

Many of our shortcomings are traceable to the peculiar developmental history of probation. In the past we have, as noted, had some difficulty in finding our legal and constitutional niche. Likewise, we have not had, until relatively recently, any well-defined place in the social work or sociomedical scheme of things. We have even been *parvenu* with the police to some extent. And we have created no end of confusion in journalistic circles. It is only twenty years or so since an editor—in Boston of all places—could so thoroughly misunderstand both the methods and the purposes of the presentence investigation that he could print in the now defunct

Transcript the following editorial about a crime which evoked one of his news column headlines:

> Last night Mrs. Blank, a young suburban matron, was removed to the city hospital with two broken legs suffered when she jumped out a second story window to escape from two men who invaded her home and attempted to assault her. Poor girl! No probation officers hasten to her bedside to comfort her. They are too busy down at the jail comforting the two thugs who attacked her.

This is a far cry from the true objective of those visits down at the jail and elsewhere: to assemble, verify, and report the information that will make the victims of crime and the whole community more comfortable and more secure in the confident knowledge that all appropriate steps are being taken to see to it that the type of conduct represented by the offense does not happen again; that the "comforting" of the duly convicted offender is accompanied by a large leavening of versatile and proven correctional disciplines, as determined by exhaustive diagnostic study.

From a social casework standpoint, then, the principal purpose of the investigation report is to provide the diagnostic information on the basis of which intelligent and workable retraining programs can be formulated and carried forward, in or out of correctional institutions. In the very nature of things, this purpose cannot be divorced from—indeed, it must always be subordinated to—the primary function of the report, which is to serve as a guide and aid to the court in determining the specific judgment. In the latter connection, there is no question that it can, and does, influence the decision of the judge. This is precisely what it is supposed to do, if one reads the language of the pertinent statutes correctly. This, in turn, is the factor which has given rise to the long series of procedural and constitutional questions which have heretofore led to certain misunderstandings of the methods of the investigation and which have finally been resolved by the United States Supreme Court.

ETHICAL OBLIGATIONS

The awesome responsibilities here entailed impose obligations of a very special nature upon the probation officer. Ours is a democratic society and the officer's authority over the object of his investigation is in no sense definitive, but to paraphrase what old Abe Martin said about poverty not being a crime, "It might just as well be." The ability or opportunity to influence the judge in the fateful disposition of the lives and liberties of other human beings has grave ethical implications which in themselves demand of the probation officer a sense of ethical balance that simply cannot afford to be less than exquisite.

Thorough documentation and a complete absence of prejudice or bias, for or against a defendant, are the elementary requisites of good report writing. This should apply especially to those items of information secured from "out of court" sources and not subjected to the refining or purifying fire of examination and cross-examination in the courtroom.

JUDICIAL AND CORRECTIONAL NEEDS

This brings us back to the "thirty prior burglaries" and the "morbid sexuality" which occasioned all the furor in the Williams case. Probation officers are interested in the evidence of criminal behavior as such, or in other "adverse" information, only to the extent that it depicts a facet or facets of the unique character of the offender. Apart from this and apart from the fact that criminal or other abnormal behavior may be the immediate expression of malignancies or other personality disorders which need to be remedied, there is no theoretical casework reason why probation reports have to dwell on these items at all. The real job is portrayal of the background of the defendant and of the interplay of his attitudes and actions with those of others, together with analysis of his motivations. All of this is consciously directed toward rechanneling those urges and inclinations which run counter to the individual and social well-being and toward eliminating or improving those factors in the external situation which may have any part in "causing" the behavior. The probation officer is not interested in punishment, except insofar as it is therapeutic, and he is certainly not interested in making the punishment fit the crime or the criminality.

The probation officer must re-examine evidence of the crime or past criminal history, principally to present a rounded picture of the defendant. The person who commits thirty successful burglaries before detection does not, for correctional purposes, constitute the same problem as the inept bungler who gets caught the first time or every time. Correctional treatment, by and large, needs a different method of application for a first offender from that which is indicated for an old repeater. In the Williams case, it was necessary to refer to the "thirty prior burglaries" because, of one thing, the probation officer reasonably expected that the life sentence (with some possibility of eventual pardon and release), rather than the death penalty, would be pronounced, in which event excluding the reference would have amounted, from a correctional standpoint, to improper concealment. Even here, the ethical obligation to report factually and objectively had to be observed.

DUE PROCESS REQUIREMENTS

The thirty prior burglaries which were not "in evidence" were therefore documented. They were supported in some instances by the defendant's own admissions; in many of these he furnished considerable descriptive embellishment. In other instances there was positive identification, beyond possibility of reasonable doubt, either directly by the victims or through the proceeds of burglaries found in the defendant's possession. Those instances in which there was neither admission nor identification were carefully described as mere allegations of which no proof had been adduced.

The reference to "morbid sexuality" was likewise not manufactured out of the investigator's imagination or out of any regard that he might have had for his own prowess as a medical or psychiatric diagnostician. The phrase itself appeared nowhere in the probation report, being instead the judge's none too felicitous condensation of the data which did appear. The basis for this characterization was furnished to the probation officer in a penetrating and lengthy medical report from the United States Army, where the defendant had been under close psychiatric observation in a rehabilitation hospital for many months. He had been diagnosed there as neither legally nor medically insane but had been described, with a wealth of clinical and other evidence, as a serious and potentially dangerous sexual deviate.

Even the allegation contained in the argument on appeal—that this defendant had not been "confronted" with the witnesses supplying adverse information against him and had not been given an opportunity for cross-examination and rebuttal—was true only to the extent that this had not been done in open court and on the record. It is, or should be, a standard probation practice to discuss with every convicted defendant such "damaging" information as may have been uncovered concerning him. This is actually an integral part of the diagnostic process, by which is meant the probing into attitudes and actions, admissions and evasions, ambitions and frustrations, emotions and mental mechanisms, and all the other elements that go to make up a picture of a personality. In the Williams case, as in every other case, the pertinent "out of court" information was discussed with the defendant at length. His reactions and explanations were reported in such a way as to distinguish between hypothesis and demonstrated fact and in such a way also as to enable the sentencing judge to decide for himself which portions of the information he would admit for sentence purposes and which he would disregard.

As a matter of fact, in most self-respecting probation agencies, the information submitted in the presentence report is never so far "out of court" as might appear at first glance. The probation officer works in a judicial atmosphere, having been hired by the court on qualifications established by the court, with responsibility directly to the court for everything he does, and at all times under the direction of the court. He has the right to assume—and experience amply justifies the assumption—that, as the judge is competent to rule upon the admissibility of evidence at trial, he is equally competent to evaluate the materiality and propriety of evidence submitted to him in a probation report.

CURRENT STANDARDS OF REPORTING

So much for the obligations imposed upon probation by ethics, by judicial and correctional needs, and by requirements of due process of law. We come now to a discussion of the current scene and of presentence reporting standards.

What has been said above may serve perhaps to point up the

essential fallacy of the often-quoted remark: "The average court takes days, sometimes weeks, to determine guilt, but only a few minutes or at most a few hours to determine treatment." Even in the traffic courts, where the imposition of the fine or the five days takes but a few seconds, the guilt-finding process ("Q. How do you plead? A. Guilty!") takes less time. In the juvenile courts, practically everywhere in the country nowadays, the determination of treatment is what consumes practically all of the time of the courts and investigating probation staffs. There the prevailing philosophy is that responsibility for the delinquent act, as well as for delinquency in the abstract, rests in the community rather than in the child. Hence, action is initiated for the most part on the basis of a petition filed in the child's behalf and not on a complaint filed against him. Accordingly, the establishment of responsibility or "guilt" is not the critical question. Something along the same line is happening in relation to adolescents and young adults, as witness the recent trend toward various types of legislative enactments and administrative schemes designed to remove the stigma of conviction of—or even of trial for—criminal or quasi-criminal offenses, and generally to modify or ameliorate the penal procedures in this area.

In the adult courts, whether of major or minor criminal jurisdiction, we have advanced to a stage where the disposition and the thought and energy expended to arrive at it are likewise coming to occupy a major portion of the time. This is true even of those notorious or "juicy" trials where the court action alone consumes days or weeks, and, incidentally, pre-empts the headlines. It is particularly true of the vast number of cases, estimated to comprise 90 per cent or more of total volume, where convictions are entered by pleas of guilty. Discounting, for our purpose here, the time and effort put into such cases by the police, grand jury, prosecutor, etc., the establishment of guilt is a relatively speedy, if inconspicuous, operation. In accepting pleas, judges usually leave the finding of the facts (including the criminal facts) which will affect or govern the disposition to the probation officer, making sure only (a) that the defendant has been fully advised of his rights; (b) that no one has coerced or inveigled him into confession; (c) that he actually did commit the act or acts alleged against him in the bald recital in the complaint or indictment; and (d) that he fully knows what he is doing in pleading guilty and is prepared to take the consequences, whatever these may be.

HOW MUCH TIME FOR A REPORT?

At this point, and usually only at this point, begins the lengthy and frequently complex study that will eventually "determine treatment." No reliable information is at hand to indicate just how much time the average good investigation requires (in the nation-wide experience, that is). It is affected by size of caseloads, paucity or multiplicity of sources of information, availability of clinical services, considerations of geography, and many other factors too numerous to mention. The experience in our own court, where we have at least a semblance of adequacy of staff in relation to volume of work (most of them fortunately still enjoying a fairly reasonable endowment of physical stamina and other such attributes, although the wear and tear and the climbing of endless flights of tenement stairs are beginning to tell), and where geographical distances are of no great moment, is that a "good" investigation and the preparation of the report thereon takes three to four weeks.

There seems to be no magic formula for speeding up the verification of vital statistics; the canvass of school, vocational, and social agency records; the digging for medical and psychiatric information; the interviews with complainants, police, witnesses, relatives, pastors, employers, the soul-searching sessions with defendants themselves. Given all sorts of administrative gadgets and other expedients to cut down on clerical chores, routine clearances, etc., the three or four weeks are still eaten up. Another week is consumed, on the average, in digesting and evaluating the findings of the investigation for purposes of working out the required formal sentence recommendation to the court. Yet another week may go by in various amplifying, clarifying, and interpreting consultations with the judge. Put under pressure, as we often are, we are able to reduce the time lapse appreciably here and there but it is doubtful that this can be done consistently without paying a price somewhere. I suppose it would be possible in this streamlined electronic

age to devise the sort of stereotyped to-be-read-while-running probation report that could be turned out on a mass-production, belt-
line-transmission basis. I hope that it can never happen here.

The time element, while important, is of far less concern than
quality. Here again, no reliable information on nation-wide standards is at hand. What evidence there is to suggest that the standards
vary greatly from place to place. In some places none exist at all.
You may remember the note of dissatisfaction, if not indeed of
exasperation, that crept from time to time into the Gluecks' *Later
Criminal Careers* and some of their other works, over the naïveté,
scantiness, or complete absence of diagnostic data, to say nothing of
research data, in the probation and institutional records they used
as the basis for their monumental studies. Joseph P. Murphy, the
able and amiable chief probation officer of Essex County, New
Jersey, in his ten-year follow-up study of probation outcomes,
found himself compelled to qualify radically many of his conclusions and comparisons, because in a substantial number of the early
cases in the samplings, probation had been granted on the basis of
either a meager presentence investigation or no investigation at
all. I myself have been told by one of our judges (not too long ago,
either) that I, and not the defendant, was the one who should be
committed to Kings County Hospital to have his head examined,
for offering suggestions on a basis of palpably incomplete findings
presented in a presentence report.

Completeness of factual information does not always fill the
bill either, qualitatively speaking. The federal probation service
has long been known for high standards. Yet, Ben Meeker, in his
scholarly *Analysis of a Presentence Report* (the report in question being, to all appearances, culled from the official files of the
federal service and not altered in any essentials) found more to
criticize than to commend. He conceded the descriptive data to
be complete enough for the most part. But he makes this incisive
observation regarding one item of the investigation (and repeats
the essence of it in a great many others) : "A person's *conception*
of the adequacy of his home may be more important in determining his reactions to that home than any objective impressions of the
adequacy or inadequacy of such a home gained by a probation
officer." If this is something for the diligent, discriminating pro-

bation officer to paste in his hat, what can one say of a fellow who clutters up the record with all sorts of irrelevant, inconsequential claptrap in the name of completeness, often without attempting at all to establish the diagnostic or therapeutic significance of these trivia?

THE PROSE OF PRESENTENCE REPORTS

On the other hand, it is possible also to do the "diagnosing" to death. One of the not uncommon occupational diseases of report writers seems to be an incapacity to credit their readers with any imagination or any critical faculty at all. Instead of marshaling and presenting the facts in such a manner that they speak for themselves, some have a compulsion to spell out laboriously the conclusions— even the obvious ones—to be derived from the facts.

Worse still, they do so in the dreadful idiom of the social case-work textbooks instead of in English. A few years ago we had a student from one of the schools of social work doing his field work in our court. At the end of a fairly tolerable report on one of the presentence investigations we assigned to him, he offered this "diagnosis" of a 45-year-old defendant who had assaulted a cop and who had been in no real trouble since his parents and the police stopped "picking on him" twenty-five years before:

> Internalizing, integrating and building upon a series of frustrating infantile and early adolescent life experiences in which his delinquent ventures were invariably met with a rigidly structured parental opposition and with quick apprehension and punishment, the memory of which appears to be reviving with the onset of the involutional phase of his life, the defendant has reverted to an initial pattern of viewing all authority figures with suspicion. His present offense clearly demonstrates an evolving or re-evolving antisocial *affect,* featured by a need for ego enhancement, as represented by the status achieved in thinking of himself as a "big shot" who will not be dominated by the police.

The student told his astonished supervisor that he had adapted this stuff from a "case illustration" which he found in a textbook, and sure enough he had! The author indicated it was an authentic quotation from a presentence report, which he apparently regarded with some favor. One wonders just what impression it was intended to make upon the court or what conceivable use it could be in the treatment process. There is, of course, the possibility that the writer of it wished to do a little judicial jaw breaking in the event His Honor might be rash enough to read the effusion aloud. This could in certain circumstances be a laudable enough forethought to nullify any possible criticism and, on that basis, I would be willing to take mine back. Fortunately, this type of "reporting" is not in high repute among probation departments generally. There are, however, enough variations of the same technique and the same type of pseudo-sophisticated verbiage floating around to suggest that probation would do well to re-examine some of its reporting practices. This sort of thing is bad enough when the conclusions, once deciphered, are found to have some relationship to the information on which they are founded. They can be devastating when they turn out to be *non sequiturs*. In all fairness, it must be conceded that, to the extent that this evil exists, it is a derivative of our indiscriminate borrowings from the terminology of the behavioral sciences. We have long had a tendency to use this borrowed language to foreshorten the more exacting avenues of case investigations, a tendency which probation administrators have done little to discourage up to now. It's about time we grew up.

FORMAT OF THE REPORT

The presentence investigation report, which is in continuous process of improvement everywhere, embraces, as of now, the following elements, which are, of course, subject to variations of emphasis, depending on the needs and facilities of the courts in the various jurisdictions but which may be regarded as minimum standard practice generally throughout the nation:

1. Present Offense: Under this heading, the offense (the one actually before the court) is described in narrative fashion. Details are given as to time, place, circumstances, and nature of the crime, with particular reference to the exact parts played by the defendant and his associates, if any. The sequence of events leading up to the arrest is portrayed, as is the manner of the arrest itself. Care is taken to give the source of each item of information, together with the names, addresses, and occupations of the complainant, witnesses, and other affected persons, and the name and command of the arresting officer. Repetition of detail is avoided, but if there is more than one version of the circumstances of the crime, the discrepancies are noted and explored. If these cannot be reconciled, they are reported as found, so that the court may determine for itself whether they are important enough to warrant clarification by testimony taking.

   2. Status of Codefendants and Accomplices: The part played by codefendants is noted in this section, together with the disposition or present status of any changes filed against them. As much information as possible is sought and reported concerning unapprehended accomplices, whether their actual identity is known or not. All of this is important in later treatment, whether in or out of prison, since criminal associates are an important factor in the life and inclinations of the subject.

   3. Statement of the Defendant: This section gives the defendant's version of his involvement in the offense. Sometimes, when convicted by verdict, defendants will make no statement at all or will vigorously deny everything and protest their innocence. The investigator accepts whatever statements they care to make, however inconsistent these may be with the facts as he otherwise knows them. This is done to preserve the defendant's rights in the event of appeal. The same procedure is followed with a special classification of young offenders coming within the purview of the Youthful Offender Act (or like statutes) who are investigated, with their written consent and that of their attorneys *before trial,* to determine whether a social purpose would be served by not taking them to trial at all. Such youths, in consenting to investigation, do not relinquish their constitutional right to presumption of innocence. Many of them do, however, talk freely if really guilty, since understanding of the beneficial purpose of the investigation (to obviate the stigma or the civil disabilities that often arise in later life from conviction of a criminal offense) is widespread. In "plea of guilty" cases, as described earlier, most defendants readily acknowledge guilt and have little hesitancy in unburdening themselves. Occasionally, however, they hedge their admissions around with all manner of evasion and rationalization. In that case, it is the probation officer's job to use his interviewing skills to cut through the make-believe and the wishful thinking and get at the facts. It is a firmly held theory of correctional work that good confession is, all by itself, an important part of rehabilitation. Consequently, the probation officer makes a special effort to get defendants to "come clean" all the way.

There are, of course, certain categories of offenders, frequently needing psychiatric assistance, who are constitutionally incapable of facing up to or acknowledging responsibility for their acts. They present a keen challenge to the professional diagnostic competency of the probation officer and have a value all their own in that connection.

While ordinarily this phase of the investigation does not have any probative force in settling any lingering questions of innocence or guilt, sometimes it is the decisive factor in resolving just such questions. In rare instances, probation officers have exculpated offenders adjudged guilty in error through flaws in the evidence or improper understanding of the court proceedings. In every case, the judge is kept informed of any snags that occur so that remedial action of one sort or another, if indicated, may be promptly taken.

4. Attitude of Complainant: Under our American system, criminal offenses are not merely personal crimes; by statutory definition, they are crimes against the whole community. Nevertheless, the complainant of record, the immediate victim of the offense, is a most important figure in the whole proceedings. His feelings with respect to disposition are reported. Sometimes, they have to be thoroughly talked through with him and sometimes fears and obsessions have to be allayed. Not infrequently, the complainant himself is a subject for rehabilitation, financially or for other reasons. Probation officers now consider this effort to be part of their function.

5. Aggravating and Mitigating Circumstances: Pertinent comment is made under this heading to such aspects or consequences of the criminal act as the following:

(a) *For All Offenses:* Premeditation or deliberation or the absence of such; whether the offender was a leader or follower or lone operator in the commission of the crime; intoxication or sobriety; resistance to arrest; cooperation with authorities in identification of confederates or in recovering proceeds of crime; apparent repentance or defiance (how sincere?) ; whether offense was an isolated episode or one of a series; whether there was provocation, real or imagined, or whether involvement was fortuitous.

(b) *For Crimes against the Person:* Use of weapons; extent of victim's injuries, permanent or temporary disfigurement, hospitalization, loss of income, etc.; aggressiveness of defendant (and perhaps also of complainant) .

(c) *For Property Crimes:* Amount of victim's financial loss or property damage; losses recovered and unrecovered; whether there was insurance coverage; economic circumstances of the complainant (sometimes as contrasted with those of the defendant) ; extent to which restitution has been or can be made; whether there was a violation of fiduciary responsibility or perhaps professional ethics on the part of the defendant.

(d) *For Sex Crimes:* Age, education, mental condition, reputation, and chastity of victim; whether a social disease was transmitted or a pregnancy ensued; disparity in ages of complainant and defendant.

The foregoing is only an outline. The factors to be described under the heading of "Aggravating and Mitigating Circumstances" are subject to a wide range of variations, depending upon a wide variety of situations; however, this entire section of the presentence investigation report should be written as concisely as possible.

6. Prior Criminal History: Listed in this section is a factual chronological record of the defendant's prior criminal history. Dates, courts, titles of offenses, and dispositions are verified from the official records and reported together with a brief description of each offense. An effort is made to ascertain and report the defendant's attitudes and feelings (in retrospect) for each prior offense, for whatever insight may be gained thereby into his criminal habits and motivations, but with as little editorializing as possible.

7. Antecedents and Family Background: Names, ages, occupations, etc., of parents are listed here, after investigation and verification. Family attitudes and relationships are explored (in the appropriate interviews) . Particular reference is made to the home atmosphere (felicity, security, health, etc.) in which the defendant has been reared. All data concerning family composition, relationships, standing in the community, etc., are carefully checked against the records of other agencies to which the family may have been known. Probation officers have ready, almost automatic, access to the records of these agencies and are under binding professional agreement to preserve the confidentiality of any information culled from them. Where indicated, neighborhood inquiries concerning the family and its members are discreetly made. All sources of information, both within and without the home, are noted in the text or marginally. Racial and national derivations are noted and, where the circumstances warrant it, the probation officer may go back into the family tree to obtain data on those factors in the family inheritance that may have had any effect upon its social conditioning or that of the defendant.

Brothers and sisters also come in for attention, with as much biographical and identifying detail on each as seems desirable. This information is of special value to prison administrators in regulating visiting privileges and as a factor in promoting prison morale. It is also a vital resource in probation supervision, particularly in cases where the subject has difficult sledding for any reason; and as a check against the possibility of later successful absconding, it is invaluable. Attitudes and relationships of the various relatives toward the defendant are gone into, as well as his toward them. Any past or present psychopathological or criminal taints are noted for whatever bearing they may have on family interrelationships or in understanding the defendent's situation with regard to them.

Where no immediate family relatives are available for interview, special efforts are made through co-operating agencies elsewhere to run them down and secure the desired verifications and other items of information. If this effort is unsuccessful or if no near relatives exist, the officer attempts to get in touch with next of kin. If the defendant requests that no contact at all be made with relatives, his motives are carefully explored. In some cases it may be expedient or even profitable to respect his wishes; the more common experience, however, is that they are best judiciously overridden.

If the defendant is married, or has been, the names, ages, and other identifying data on spouses and ex-spouses are recorded, as are those of children resulting from the unions. Appropriate verifications are made of marriages, separations, and divorces. Defendant's record as a provider is examined, as are the causes of any incompatability. Spouses and ex-spouses are always interviewed, but approaches to children, especially minor children, are always delicately undertaken.

8. Developmental History of the Defendant:

(a) *Early Developmental History:* All ascertainable data with reference to gestation and to pathology at birth or in infancy are recorded in this section, together with clinically significant incidents of the period.

(b) *School Period:* A verified record of conduct and performance at elementary school is secured from all the schools the defendant attended. The highlights of other phases of the defendant's life at this period are also woven into the narrative.

(c) *Adolescent Period:* High school or college history, if any, is obtained and recorded. Stresses and strains of adolescent adjustments are explored and reported. If the defendant was employed in this period, the necessary verifications are made with appropriate data on earnings, skills, job adjustments and tenures, earning capacity, savings, etc. Information on continuing educational needs and vocational aptitudes and goals begins to become important at this stage, as do avocational interests and associations outside the home.

(d) *Adult History:* The same type of information as for the adolescent period is carried forward into this stage. Military service is verified, as is membership in trade unions, fraternal organizations, etc.

Throughout the recital of the details of the defendant's life, as portrayed in this section and elsewhere in the report, the significance of the various developments to the defendant himself is kept in focus; since, as Meeker points out, the really relevant elements in any diagnostic study are not the objective impressions of the investigators but the offender's attitudes and reactions to events and individuals.

9. Residence Arrangements: This section is devoted to a description of the home surroundings of the defendant at the time of arrest and the period immediately preceding it. The physical ar-

rangement, rent, furnishing, etc., are described with particular attention to atmosphere. If the defendant owns the home, its value and his equity in it are recorded.

10. Religion: Reference is made to the defendant's interest in and attitude toward religious observance. If he has been baptized, confirmed, etc., the appropriate certificates are examined and the details noted. Where the findings disclose a need for stimulation, the pastor is visited or the cooperation of the family is sought. If the defendant is unaffiliated with or has defected from any organized religious group, an exhaustive effort is made to ascertain what ethical or other standards serve him in lieu of a religious belief.

11. Mental and Physical Health: The general health of the defendant throughout his life is discussed in this section, with especial reference to any serious illnesses or hospitalization he may have undergone. Results of recent physical or mental examinations, intelligence test, etc., are assembled in verified form. In courts having their own clinical psychiatric facilities, almost all defendants undergo some form of psychiatric diagnostic testing; the other courts do the best they can in this direction. In all courts, whether served by house clinics or not, it is fairly standard practice to refer all defendants whose criminal conduct has been abnormal *in se* for extended psychiatric observation, on an inpatient basis, which sometimes lasts for weeks. The statutes make such referrals mandatory for certain categories of offenders as a prerequisite to sentence.

Separate reports are usually furnished to the courts by the examining psychiatrists on all such referrals. It is always well to introduce such reports, in condensed form if necessary, into the probation report proper. Other psychiatric referrals are made where necessary or desirable and where the facilities permit, on a voluntary basis, if possible, and by formal order of the court, if necessary. With or without such referrals, the records of other agencies are always scrutinized for medical and psychiatric data on the defendant and members of his family. Special attention is paid throughout the presentence investigation to remediable physical defects and also to any organic or other ailments that may have in any way influenced the defendant's behavior.

12. *Character, Habits, and Associations:* This is a rather un-wieldy title which some probation departments, including ours, give to the evaluative summary and analysis of the factual information heretofore reported.

As a general rule, the diagnostic (as distinguished from the fact-gathering) interview with the defendant is deferred until the investigator can face his subject with an already verified accumulation of data on his whole background. It is much easier, under such circumstances, to appraise his statements, to ward off any attempts to take the interview into unproductive or erratic channels, and in general to get down to "brass tacks." At this point the defendant is "confronted" with both the favorable and unfavorable information that has been uncovered concerning him, and is given the opportunity to accept, explain, evade, or reject whatever is discussed. It is at this point also that he is briefed on the purposes of the investigation and prepared for as philosophical an acceptance as possible of his current and projected situation.

There is no ready format into which a description of this section of the presentence report may be compressed. The content may be, and usually is, as varied as the idiosyncrasies of the given defendant or the ramifications of his activities. Much depends also on the diagnostic and reportorial skills of the investigator. The idea is to evoke insights and perceptions into the defendant's motivations and potentials, as far as possible out of his own reactions to the matters presented to him.

As a professional person, the investigator is also expected to analyze the objective data presented to him during the entire investigation. As far as possible, the sources and authorities should be given for all conclusions reached. The rules permit impressions to be given out of the investigator's training or experience, or out of his intuitive reasoning, but they must always be clearly labeled as such.

The foregoing is an abridged outline of the basic elements of a presentence investigation. While it may not be the last word on the subject, it has been carefully tested over the years and has given satisfactory service in many jurisdictions. Whatever its imperfections, it can insure with reasonable certainty that the selection of offenders for placement on probation is not a blind gamble or an unwarranted imposition on the community. It can insure also that if offenders do go to prison, at least they go there as something more than numbers on a shirt, or card indexes in a file, and that the prison administration is in a position, if it sets its mind to the task, to get out of each individual commitment whatever creative values are there to get.

4

INTERVIEWING CANDIDATES FOR PROBATION*

A PRIME RESPONSIBILITY of the probation officer in adult investigation work is the preparation of a good presentence report for the court. The chief tool-in-trade used in accomplishing this is the personal interview with the defendant. An important prerequisite to the use of the interview is that the probation officer first understand its functioning, potential, and means of control in order to employ it effectively.

THE WORK SHEET AND INTERVIEWING

Most probation departments have developed or adapted some sort of guide and recording form for use in interviewing. Commonly known as the "work sheet," it usually consists of questions, tabular headings, and check-off items. The work sheet is a handy and convenient instrument for interviewing; it serves as a guide and a reminder to see that basic information is procured and provides a suitable method of recording such data. It also assists the officer in discussing or dictating his case as do "notes" serve a public speaker. The most diligent use of hammer and saw does not necessarily result in good carpentry and mere possession of the most elaborate "notes" does not insure a good speech presentation. In like manner, a properly and carefully filled-out work sheet does not necessarily indicate a fruitful interview. If merely asking the questions suggested by the work sheet and recording the answers would be the substance of an interview, then could not any clerk without training or even interest in the correctional field, easily conduct such an "interview" and produce a neatly typed worksheet or report?

Obviously, something else must come out of the interview besides the work sheet: almost every investigating officer in the field has at some time or other run into the following frustrating experience which points up this fact. An investigator is taken ill or some emergency situation arises; he is unable to complete the case

---

*Chester H. Bartoo: *Federal Probation,* 25:19-28, 1961.

he is investigating. One of his colleagues is asked to take over. Even though the original officer has very carefully filled out the work sheet, the new officer is at a loss to proceed with the case without interviewing the defendant because the work sheet, with all its checks, questions, and filled-in spaces, is only a piece of cold writing and in itself conveys no vibrant picture of the defendant, his personality, attitudes, reactions, and potential. Such vital insights come from the interviewing experience itself and are not reducible to mere notations on a work sheet. If interviewing is more than merely filling out a work sheet, it would then seem wise to inquire into the process further. What is the purpose of the interview; what goals do we hope to achieve; how do we achieve them?

WHY DO WE INTERVIEW?

The first purpose of the interview is fact-finding—gathering information about the person the court has asked us to investigate. Generally, we start our interview by knowing only the defendant's name, the offense for which he was convicted, and the date on which he is to appear in court for sentence. What kind of a person is the defendant? What is his background, his outlook, his plans for the future, the things which motivate his behavior, the problems that baffle him? Where do we start in seeking answers to these questions? Rather obviously, why not with the defendant himself? We will interview him personally, ask him questions, and observe his reactions, all for the purpose of gathering information about the defendant and his world—information which will serve as the basis for our investigation report for the court.

The second purpose of the interview is to establish a "diagnosis." A physician will not attempt to prescribe treatment for a patient until he has diagnosed the condition. Like the doctor, we must first observe and study a person's symptoms and establish the nature and extent of his ailment before we can suggest a course of treatment.

Another purpose of the interview is to determine the chances of a favorable response to probation supervision. Are facilities adequate for dealing with the defendant's particular problems and needs? Does he possess the capacity to benefit from the treatment facilities available? Does he appear properly motivated? Does he recognize and accept the need for change? Does he possess the degree of mental, physical, social, and emotional maturity necessary to undertake such a program? We seek answers to such questions to assist us in determining the likelihood of his adjustment on probation and to help the court to decide what disposition to make in the respective case.

WHAT ARE OUR GOALS IN INTERVIEWING?

To know what we are trying to accomplish in an interview, we must first establish those goals for which we strive. Since two persons are involved in the interview (the probation officer and the defendant), we must recognize that two sets of goals are involved, that the goals for each of them will differ, and, since it is the probation officer who initiates and conducts the interview, that both sets of goals will be established by him. What, then, are to be the goals for each?

Some Goals for the Probation Officer: Certainly one of the primary goals is to *get information* from and about the defendant. We want to know all about him; what he can tell us; how he thinks, feels, reacts; his background, education, outlook on life; his attitudes, social and moral values, ambitions; his strengths and weaknesses; his story; his plans for the future. In short, we want all the information he can give us and all the pertinent data we can gather through observation and personal contact with him.

This, in turn, suggests another important goal: *To get acquainted with the defendant.* How well we achieve our first goal depends largely on how well we achieve this second goal. Until we establish a friendly relationship and willing participation on the part of the defendant, we will experience difficulty in obtaining satisfactory answers to our questions.

Another important goal for the probation officer is *to prepare the defendant* for what lies ahead. Whatever this might be, the experience is bound to be more meaningful to him if he is prepared for it, understands it, and accepts it in the proper perspective.

Some Goals for the Defendant: Since the primary goal of the probation officer is to secure information from and about the defendant, then a primary goal we establish for the defendant is to *provide information* about himself.

Another significant goal is that the defendant be given an opportunity for a productive experience which will be beneficial and enlightening to him. This can be achieved by helping him gain insight into and understanding of his own behavior problems and encouraging him to actively participate in their solution. The defendant should also be encouraged to examine his own strengths and weaknesses, to realize his potentials, and to recognize where he can utilize outside help or guidance through referrals to community agencies and resources for vocational guidance, marital counseling, budgeting, and psychotherapy.

WHAT ABOUT ATTITUDES?

An important factor to consider during the interview is that of attitudes—both the defendant's and our own. Attitudes expressed by the defendant are bound to color and affect our relationships with him. Just as significant are our own attitudes. It would be well for all of us to first examine our own attitudes about the defendant, his personality, and the nature of his offense. Will we be authoritative? Will we be an avenger or crusader? Will our attitude imply a role of an implacable censor or suggest that of a helpful friend and counselor? What effect will our attitude have on our questions and the responses the defendant gives to them?

Even though we may recognize and understand our own attitudes, we cannot expect to predict what will be the attitudes and reactions of the person we interview until we are in the interview situation. But we can anticipate some of the reactions and responses so that we can at least be prepared. For instance, what will be our course of action if the defendant is belligerent, or has a chip on his shoulder? Or if he is negative, apathetic, wary, doubtful, loquacious, taciturn?

We must not overlook the fact that attitudes affect one another. A warm, friendly attitude will encourage another and strengthen rapport. On the other hand, if the probation officer's attitude suggests that he expects hostility from the defendant, negative barriers are amplified and rapport is delayed. This suggests another interview goal, namely, to create in the defendant's mind, through our own attitude, that the probation officer is at least one person in authority who is friendly and will listen understandingly.

CONTROLLING THE INTERVIEW

Control of an interview in an authoritative setting obviously rests with the person in authority. Should the defendant be allowed to express whatever he feels? Or should he only answer specifically the questions asked by the probation officer? Achieving a "golden mean" would be preferable to either of these extremes. In probation interviews, especially, this would seem the most practical and productive approach.

Caseloads, deadlines, and limitations of time preclude the probation officer's use of completely nondirective interviewing; yet, in reviewing the goals we have already discussed, it would seem we cannot hope to achieve them if we limit ourselves largely to direct-questioning methods. We must obtain certain information from the defendant within the time limits of the interview. The practical approach in most cases, it would seem, is to ask him a sequence of questions which will encourage him to supply the information sought as specifically and objectively as possible. Nevertheless, within the time available, we can in our questioning, attitude, demeanor, and understanding, encourage the defendant to amplify and fully express his feelings. The probation officer must exercise his professional judgment as to what point and to what extent he must direct the course of the interview in order to get "back on beam."

HOW SHALL WE APPROACH THE INTERVIEW?

Ideally, interviews should be friendly, well-mannered, and courteous. In many instances the defendant approaches an interview with trepidation, uncertainty, and fear of the unknown future ahead. He wonders who the probation officer is, what type of a person he is, what reactions and responses on his part will prove most beneficial to him. He is, therefore, usually defensive, possibly antagonistic, and frequently, is totally without knowledge of the nature, extent, and significance (to him) of the probation process. Often he waits for the probation officer's initial move to determine what his own attitudes and responses will be.

The probation officer, on the other hand, knows his goals, is familiar with the interview procedure, and possesses the authority, training, and experience to control the interview situation. He can project himself into "the other fellow's place" and may be able to determine what may ease the defendant's mind and his tensions. In general, the steps he takes are the following:

(1) Introduces himself.

(2) Explains the purpose of the interview and what probation is, thus relieving the defendant of any fears and misgivings he might have.

(3) Helps the defendant to see what part the defendant will play during the interview and what lies ahead.

(4) Helps the defendant feel that the probation officer is someone in authority who will listen to him sympathetically and understandingly and try to help him with his problems.

SOME INTERVIEW SUGGESTIONS

It is not within the scope of this article to give a detailed discussion of "how to interview." Most department manuals provide ample material and instruction on the mechanics of the interview process. Literature on this specific subject is extensive. I should like, however, to close with some practical hints which I have chosen to call the "didactic dozen." They are based on my own experience and have been found to be helpful during the interview.

(1) In interviewing a defendant who is not in custody it is especially important that the probation officer always meet his appointment on time. If the probation officer does not keep his appointments on schedule, how can we expect the defendant to consider them important? On the other hand, some probation officers are annoyed and irritated when the defendant is not on time for the interview!

(2) Objectives should be set up ahead of time. Know what you want to accomplish and plan accordingly.

(3) Consider and evaluate the meaning of the defendant's attitudes, reactions, demeanor, speech, and problems as he explains them. Then watch for possible clues to his needs and how they may be resolved.

(4) Display a genuine interest in what the defendant has to tell. When any statement or situation is not clear, do not demand or threaten. Rather, by sympathetic concern, encourage him to ex-

plain further so that you, who want to help him, can clearly understand the entire picture he is trying to construct for you. He should not feel you doubt him or are trying to "show him up," but that you are truly interested in him and are trying to understand what he is telling you. To any indication of doubt or stern authority, he will be on the defensive; to a display of genuine interest in his welfare, he will be encouraged to cooperate fully and tell more about his true self.

(5) Wherever possible use open questions in preference to leading ones. Leading questions result in less responsive answers. A question: "Don't you like your father," or, "You don't seem to like your father much, do you?" will almost always generate a defensive answer. A more meaningful answer will likely come from a question such as: Tell me something about your father." This type of question gives a maximum range for the defendant's answer without "tipping the probation officer's hand."

(6) Carefully observe the defendant's behavior and attitudes for clues to possible problems and concerns. Where does he block, "beat around the bush," and evade? What the defendant is careful not to say often is more revealing than what he actually does say.

(7) Maintain a sincere, sympathetic, and understanding attitude. Such a relationship with the defendant makes it easier for him to disclose and discuss problems with which he has difficulty to cope.

(8) Avoid creating in the defendant's mind any notion that you are trying to "trap him"! Never lead him up a blind alley and then leave him—always leave him "an avenue of escape"! It is far better to allow the defendant to experience "a near miss" in not being entirely truthful and open with the probation officer than to force the issue and show him up as a liar! An example, not too uncommon, is the following: The defendant is asked about prior arrests and denies any. The probation officer then confronts him with identification bureau information of a previous arrest some years ago in another state. If left here, the defendant is shown to be untruthful and gone is any real hope for rapport at this point—you are now an enemy; you have deliberately shown him up! Such a situation can perhaps be avoided if the probation officer "takes the ball" at this point and affords the defendant the "avenue of escape." He might say, for example, "I am afraid I gave you the

wrong idea, Mr. Smith, in phrasing my question. I perhaps did not make myself clear. You probably thought I was referring merely to any other arrests in this city." This device avoids a showdown, gives the defendant a chance to gratefully correct himself, and, further, helps him to realize the value of telling the truth. The fact that the defendant may be well aware of the subterfuge does not lessen its value, and, in fact, may result in greater respect for the probation officer, generating even a closer bond between the two.

(9) At all times be friendly, courteous, and understanding, but beware of overidentification with the defendant. Be easy, free, and sympathetic and keep your speech and demeanor on a professional plane. Avoid pretentiousness and neither allow yourself to drop into vulgarity nor coarseness of speech, nor "talk over the defendant's head"! Do not be led into a discussion of the defendant's innocence or guilt, or commiserate with him on the findings of the court. Above all, avoid the cardinal sin of retrying the defendant's case with him, during the interview or later in the probation report!

(10) The probation officer should avoid "taking over for the defendant"! It is very important to the interview situation that the defendant recognizes and accepts his problem as his own and acknowledges the need to do something about it.

(11) It is important to keep in mind that the probation interview is primarily an instrument designed to discover, develop, and deal with the problems and needs of the defendant; hence, the probation officer is never justified in using it to seek satisfaction of his own ego-needs! Tongue-lashing a defendant, a tendency to moralize, a feeling that we "told the defendant off" are clear indications of blindspots in our personality make-up. The prudent officer is ever watchful to detect any of these symptoms within himself.

(12) It is important that the probation officer establish and maintain stability and perspective throughout his relationships with the defendant! Remember always that interviewing is a give-and-take process; the probation officer wants information for a diagnosis and treatment plan while the defendant wants information for selfhelp, and understanding. The interview is an integral part of the overall treatment process; it *is* treatment. It should give

the defendant a feeling of greater security and greater insight into his own behavior. It also should encourage him to establish acceptable and worthwhile goals for his own future development.

In conclusion, we are reminded that our interviews form the basis of the investigation report which will assist the court to determine what type of disposition is for the best interests of the defendant, his family, and the community at large. Hence, developing and improving our interviewing skills and techniques will tend to increase the quality and effectiveness of such reports and enable us to do a better job for the community.

5

PRISON OR PROBATION—WHICH AND WHY*

Every responsible citizen, as well as every judge, is deeply concerned, indeed shocked, by the crime wave sweeping the country like a deadly plague to threaten the very life of our ordered society. From the pulpit to the Halls of Congress, from the fireside of the responsible parent to the local civic clubs; from the sociologist and welfare workers to the employer of labor, comes the cry for protection from the marauding criminal. Crime and criminals are denounced everywhere, but any attempted discussion of remedial measures leads inevitably to an irreconcilable conflict of opinion. With every atrocious crime, the affected community clamors for harsher punishment. And, unfortunately, most of those who clamor for more stringent penalties as a solution to criminality seldom have the responsibility for enforcing the law or imposing the sentence, and know nothing of the background or mental capacity of the offender. It is those in the main who today decry the use of probation or any other form of treatment outside of the prison wall as maudlin sentimentality of the social worker and psychic ruminations of the psychiatrist.

It is in this atmosphere of consternation and unenlightenment that judges and prosecutors undertake the task of administering criminal justice for the protection and well-being of an ordered society. In the discharge of those important functions of government they act as public servants and as instrumentalities of their constituency. As such they may not be insensible to the emotional reactions of the community. But they also have a higher duty to exercise an informed independent judgment for the public good. It is the discharge of this duty which we hope to inspire and encourage by exchange of ideas and experiences.

Since the inception of an ordered society, we have been busily engaged in the process of making rules for the determination of

*Alfred Murrah: The Journal of Criminal Law, *Criminology, and Police Science,* 47:451-55, 1956.

guilt and innocence. The sentencing judge need only turn his hand for authoritative rules for the conduct of the trial of a criminal case. Yet, only recently have we given any consideration to the sentencing function of the judicial process. And with good reason, for when death or eye for an eye was the only penalty, the function of imposing the sentence involved no discretion—the offense determined the penalty without regard to responsibility or culpability. But, a more civilized appraisal of the offender as part of his community and the recognition that after all, he is the product of ordered society, has led us gradually to the notion that humane treatment outside prison walls has a definite place in our criminal jurisprudence; that scientific analysis of the offender, not emotional recompense, is the more effective corrective procedure. With this new concept, an added responsibility has come to the judiciary and particularly those charged with the sentencing function. And we literally grope for guides along the way. It is startling to note that in this great civilized country, the authority of a federal judge to suspend a sentence and grant probation was first given by Congress in 1925, after much agitation and controversy.

In his address to the annual meeting of the American Law Institute the Chief Justice of the United States emphasized the importance of probation in the Federal system, saying "The public and even our own profession know altogether too little about it as a factor in the administration of criminal justice." And, there are other worth-while studies by the social scientists on whose advice and counsel we are slowly but surely learning to rely. All of this indicates an aroused interest in the problem confronting a judge charged with the responsibility of imposing sentence after guilt has been established.

Let us consider for a moment some of the suggested considerations which should enter into the imposition of a sentence. At the outset, we must lay to one side as not within our competence, the vast number of criminal cases wherein the jury is the final arbiter, not only of guilt or innocence, but the extent of punishment as well. In those cases punishment is determined by the imponderables of courtroom psychology, depending upon the jurors' individual concept of punishment to fit the crime. Without having access to the deliberations in the jury room, we know that the degree of punishment is oftimes a compromise between those who would hang and those who would acquit. In those cases the judge has no responsibility and the sentencing process is purely perfunctory.

And, we must also lay aside that vast number of criminal cases wherein the extent of punishment is determined across the bargaining table of the prosecutor, with the prosecutor on one side and the defense attorney or public defender on the other, the prosecutor contending that he cannot only secure conviction, but a long sentence as well, and the defense attorney making equally extravagant claims. The result is a compromise in which the offender agrees to plead guilty to a sentence which may or may not fit the crime or the offender. In those cases, the plea and agreement are announced in court and the judge usually follows the recommendation with formal pronouncement of the sentence. The defendant is ordinarily fully informed of the bargaining process and goes off to prison thinking that he made a pretty good trade with the society he has wronged.

Let us hope that the day is not far when the responsibility for the imposition of sentence after the establishment of guilt shall rest upon the broad shoulders of a conscientious judge who approaches the discharge of his inescapable duty with the concept that in the analysis, rehabilitation, not retribution and revenge, is the prime objective of a sentence; that rehabilitation is seldom achieved by the imposition of punitive punishment; and that no man should be sent to a penal institution until it is definitely determined that he is not a fit subject for probation. Until that day comes, we must content ourselves with the practical considerations available to us as representatives of a society which has not yet reached that stage of civilization which will enable us to discharge our sentencing function on the same scientific basis now employed in the detection and apprehension of the offender.

Assuming, therefore, that probation is available to the sentencing judge, when and why should it be granted? Two factors usually enter into the determination of whether or not an offender will be placed on probation, one, the nature of the offense, the other, the nature of the offender. The criminologist would first consider the nature and character of the offender, but most judges, either consciously or unconsciously, usually consider first the offense and then the offender. There are judges who, respecting the tenor of the community and society which they represent, hold to the idea that certain offenses are not probationable, regardless of the circumstances under which they were committed or the nature of the offender. And, as a further reflection of this social attitude, many legislatures have seen fit to prescribe mandatory prison sentences for certain offenses. The sentencing records of many judges, as well as their own statements, show "highly subjective factors and personal biases in the imposition of sentence."

There are undoubtedly certain offenses which in their nature are not probationable, such as certain classes of sex crimes. Not because of the nature of the offense, but because of the nature of the offender. Then there are those offenses which are not probationable, not because of their nature, but because probation would tend to impair public respect for law. The court is not likely to place a bank robber on probation although he may be a first offender and otherwise fit for rehabilitation. We know that certain crimes of violence are committed impulsively by men of previous good character who we know are not likely to ever again threaten the safety of the community. And then there is the embezzler and the violator of public trust. We know that the judge could confidently return them to society without hazard to the community. The stigma of the crime itself is punishment enough, but the judge is nevertheless constrained to impose imprisonment, not only as a deterrent, but to satisfy the community's outraged sense of justice or to vindicate its standards of public morality. Public opinion, constructively and adroitly used, is often an aid in the sentencing process. In the language of Glueck, "While the judge must not allow public or private demands for vindictive punishment to sway him toward undue severity, he must not, on the other hand, allow the advanced thought of science to sway him toward a degree of clemency that might shock the public conscience and bring the processes of law into disrespect."

There is of course a great mass of criminal offenses in which the public has no aroused interest, and in which the judge is free to exercise his own informed judgment in the performance of the sentencing function. Even apart from public sentiment, a learned judge knows that certain offenses are so revolting and incomprehensible as to require permanent incapacitation. He also knows that probation is not intended for the professional criminal who makes his living by lawless pursuits, such as those of the narcotic peddler, professional thief, confidence man, fence, pick pocket, swindler, gangster and racketeer. They are a menace to society and it is the duty of the court to protect society by isolation or even elimination.

On the other hand, an informed judge knows that more than ninety per cent of the offenders sentenced to imprisonment return to society, most of them within two or three years, faced with the difficult task of readjusting themselves to normal habits. And, the judge also knows that the path of a great majority of these prisoners leads inevitably back to prison for offenses more atrocious than the former ones. An experienced judge knows that a first offender is not for that reason alone eligible for probation. No one has a license to violate the law one time without fear of punishment. There are undoubtedly some first offenders for whom short terms of imprisonment are not only a benefit to the community, but to the offender as well. Most judges accept the premise that a prior offender is not for that reason an unfit subject for probation. Statistics show that many second and third offenders are redeemed from a life of crime through the good judgment, faith and perseverance of the judge and the application of the wise and compassionate friendship of a dedicated probation officer.

But the resolution of all these imponderables in determining whether the judgment shall be prison or probation taxes the wisdom of a Solomon. By what standards, guides or criteria shall the judge arrive at his tremendously important decision? Some judges choose to call it ingenuity, wisdom, experience, knowledge of human nature, and relying upon that alone, claim to possess some magic power of divination by which they look into the mind and soul of the prisoner before them, and come up with a sentence which meets the ends of justice. Others call this approach the "hunch system," which "cannot be justified as a substitute for a thorough study of the individual characteristics and problems of the prisoner." There will always be an indispensable need for the analytical skill and judicial acumen in the imposition of sentence, but no amount of wisdom or discernment can take the place of factual background and diagnostic study. Statistics prove it and most judges now concede it.

How best then can the sentencing judge be apprised of all this essential data? Judge William Campbell, a great judge of one of the busiest courts in the land, says, "of all the administrative aids available to the judge an adequate, comprehensive and complete presentence investigation is the best guide to intelligent sentencing. The evaluation, interpretation and conclusions reached by a highly trained, widely experienced probation officer possessed of a high sense of integrity, a keen understanding of human behavior and great skill in the collection and appraisal of information from many sources is of utmost value." "The presentence report," continues Judge Campbell "can and should be a most thoroughgoing document involving the entire social, economic and psychological background of the offender." In recognition of this sound philosophy, the Federal Rules of Criminal Procedure provide that unless the court directs otherwise, a presentence investigation and report containing information about the offender's prior criminal record, his characteristics and financial condition, and circumstances affecting his behavior, and such other information as may be helpful in imposing sentence, shall be submitted to the court prior to sentence.

But the probation officer's duties do not end with the submission of the presentence report. If probation is granted, the probationer becomes the responsibility of the officer. He is the friend and confidant of the probationer—all of the probationer's troubles and all of his problems are laid at his feet; the officer stands between him and the community and between him and the judge. The most gratifying experience in the career of a judge is the dedicated interest and perseverance of his probation officers. These fine public servants are giving their lives and their talents to the piecing together of broken lives and making them into useful citizens. Certainly nothing can be more important to the preservation of our social structure today. A fine probation officer told me the other day that he never "lost a case" as he called it, that he "could not have won" if he had the time to give the probationer. From other sources we know that many revocations result from lack of proper supervision, and that probation is often denied because of the unavailability of proper probation supervision.

Up until very recently, the Congress and the legislatures reflecting the public suspicion of probation, have been niggardly with appropriations for the support of the probation service, and we have also been reluctant to provide adequate salaries for probation officers. There is still evidence of parsimony in this respect. When it is pointed out that the cost of maintaining a federal probationer is 26.9¢ per day or $98.26 per year, and that the cost of confinement in the penitentiary is $3.41 per day or $1243.19 per year; and that the average yearly earning of a federal probationer is $2,649.25, to say nothing of what it cost to support a convict's family while he is in prison, there can be no defense to the denial of adequate probation service or the revocation of a probation because of lack of supervision by a capable probation officer.

What we need to do as judges and interested citizens is to educate ourselves. We need to keep abreast of the advancement of the social sciences and learn to utilize their services in the performance of our high duties. Just as we have followed the psychiatrist in the repudiation of right and wrong for criminal responsibility, so should we follow the scientists in the rehabilitation of those found criminally responsible. Franz Alexander, a psychoanalyst, and Hugo Staub, a lawyer, collaborated to say: "Only when the community, in its dealings with the criminal, will become ready to give up the gratification of those affects which demand expiation, retaliation and compensation for the socially inhibited sadism, only then will our sense of justice find itself in harmony with a purely rational and scientifically sound treatment of the lawbreaker. We must find some way to combine socially indispensable punishment with the psychiatrists' knowledge and help. We need to open our judicial eyes to the established fact that the solution to lawlessness is not to be found in bigger and stronger prisons, but in reclamation through scientific research and application of humane treatment. We have made a good start but we have only scratched the surface, and time is running out.

6

PROBATIONARY SUPERVISION: CONTENTS, PERSONNEL AND ORGANIZATION*

T HE ESSENCE OF the probation system lies in the fact that the offender is not merely given "another chance," but that society provides him with constructive assistance in his struggle for social rehabilitation. It is this "element of constructive treatment in probation supervision which places probation . . . beyond either leniency or punishment." For this constructive assistance, primarily provided through the intermediary of the probation officer, the conventional term *supervision* has come to be "nothing but an expedient abbreviation". The term, in fact, is a misleading one in so far as it emphasizes only the disciplinary aspect of release on probation—the element of authoritative control over the behavior of the probationer, with the sanctions of the law and the threat of the application of suspended punishment behind it. The term probationary *supervision* betrays the historical origins of the practice which it designates—its present-day connotation is certainly much wider in scope than is implicit in the term. In its simplest form, it involves the designation of special officers (either paid or volunteer workers) to "advise, assist and befriend" the probationer. In its most complex and advanced forms, it is a process of treatment, founded on the psychological and social sciences, and consciously undertaken as a field of professional activity. In either case, it depends for its success on "a personal relationship of trust and guidance," and involves the systematic mobilization of community resources to facilitate and advance the social rehabilitation of the probationer.

While supervision is the essence of the probation system, the effectiveness of the probation services of any given country is equally dependent upon the systematic and wise selection of offenders for release on probation. It is not difficult to discern the complemen-

*Probation and Related Measures, New York, United Nations, Department of Social Affairs, E/CN/.5/230, pp. 243–256, 267–271.

69

tary nature of the two techniques. The success of probationary supervision depends to a very large extent on the original selection of probationers who are amenable to this type of treatment. Conversely, however, no measure of careful selection of probationers can compensate for inadequate supervision. Effective supervision is the goal towards which the discriminating selection of probationers is directed. It is, in the final analysis, the determining criterion by which the whole system is defined and evaluated.

THE SCOPE AND CONTENTS OF PROBATIONARY TREATMENT

The scope of the probation officer's function in relation to the probationer under his supervision is determined by the objectives of probationary supervision itself. It is generally agreed that probationary supervision is *not* primarily designed to *control* the conduct of the probationer in such a way that he does not commit any further offences. Probationary supervision is of limited duration, and the negative function of control could therefore only be exercised for the duration of the probation period. In looking beyond the duration of the actual period of supervision, it is therefore necessary to direct probationary treatment towards the permanent regeneration of the probationer's attitude towards, and capacity for, law observance. It is not possible, however, to isolate an individual's proclivity or incentives towards violating the law from the total picture of his personal characteristics and social relationships. It is inevitable therefore that probationary treatment should be concerned with the total configuration of the offender's personality in relationship to family, community and society. "The object of probation is the ultimate re-establishment of the probationer in the community and the probation officer must accordingly take a long view."

If the social rehabilitation of the offender is accepted as the object of probationary treatment, it follows that the probation officer's task is a twofold one. On the one hand, he has to deal with the probationer as an entity—his personal needs and requirements (material, medical, psychological, and social) ; his attitudes, ambitions, hopes and fears; his reaction patterns and the mainsprings of his behavior. On the other hand, and at the same time, the probation officer has to deal directly with the social setting in which the probationer is expected to function—family relationships and home circumstances, neighbourhood and recreation, school or employment, etc. Probation has this dual approach in common with social work in general. The task in question is not limited to the reshaping of the individual or to the reshaping of his social environment, but partakes of both, each within its own set of inevitable limitations.

The direct role of the probation officer in the total process of the social rehabilitation of the offender must necessarily be limited. It is obvious that the officer himself cannot adequately deal with either the personal or the environmental aspect of the problem as a whole. It is therefore necessary on the one hand to direct attention to the main difficulties in the situation of the individual offender and, on the other hand, to act as an organizer or intermediary between the probationer and the resources already available in the community.

The resources available in the community include public assistance, public health facilities, hospitals, clinics, employment exchanges, voluntary social welfare organizations offering specialized services of a varied nature, clubs and similar organizations, religious agencies, etc. The probation officer has to keep informed with reference to available resources, and has to maintain the necessary contacts to facilitate the constructive utilization of the services offered. In addition to organized services, both public and voluntary, the resources available in the community also include the goodwill, support and co-operation of individuals and private concerns. In this connection the probation officer can sometimes enlist the personal interest of teachers, leaders of civic organizations, members of service clubs, etc., to aid the probationer in working out his social readjustments.

As has already been noted, constructive probationary treatment may take place at various levels, ranging from the most simple, at which probation officers "advise, assist and befriend" probationers as occasion demands, to a level at which probationary treatment becomes a highly systematic and skilled operation. Irrespective of the level at which it takes place, however, the process has certain elements in common. The essential nature of the process is the

attempt to find forms and methods of assistance to suit the individual needs of the probationer—the differences relate to the degree of
skill and insight with which the situation is diagnosed, with
which available specialized resources are utilized, and with which
direct guidance and assistance are provided. As skill and training
increase, probation officers generally devote less time to administrative and organizational functions—such as securing various services for the probationer, etc.—and devote more attention to more
deep-seated personality problems.

Probationary treatment requires some measure of deliberate
planning. The degree to which the various features of the total situation can be consciously manipulated with a view to specific ends,
will naturally vary with the degree of training and skill represented
by the probation officer, but the process should never be completely
devoid of conscious direction on the part of the latter. On the other
hand, no "diagnosis" of a complex social and psychological configuration is ever final, and the "plan" of treatment should remain
flexible and should be varied according to circumstances and, particularly, according to the reactions of the probationer to the supervision process.

The essentials of a plan of probationary treatment in a highly
developed and professionalized probation department have been
well formulated as follows:

> The plan of treatment, if it is to have any constructive value,
> must be based upon insight into the personality and environ-
> ment of the offender. The problems he presents must be set
> forth and there must be an evaluation of the problem in terms
> of his social liabilities and assets. There must be an analysis of
> the causal factors, a definite evaluation of the probationer's
> needs, and the practical and workable means that are to be used
> to influence him toward a higher level of responsibility and social
> consciousness. . . . The plan must envisage the development of
> discipline and self control, and, whenever necessary, emotional
> adjustment and physical rehabilitation. It must apply itself also
> to academic and vocational education and religious develop-
> ment and must portray the means which are to be used for the
> development of new resources and outlets.
>
> The plan of treatment must further envisage the broadening
> of social relationships, family adjustment, and improvement in

the physical conditions under which the probationer lives, and bring about the development of a measure of financial security through the development of economic efficiency and a thrifty disbursement of earnings.

The Supervisor-Probationer Relationship as an Instrument of Treatment

The value of probationary supervision—and frequently, therefore, the success or failure of probation—depends primarily on the nature and quality of the *personal relationship* established between the probation officer and the probationer. The type of personal relationship established between probation officer and probationer varies very considerably according to the basic motivation and attitudes of the probation officer, and according to the skill and insight with which the relationship is used for specific purposes. In practice, a great variety of motives may play a part in leading probation officers to undertake their task of human salvage. In the early phases of the development of probation in England and in Massachusetts, religious considerations played a very significant part. Similarly, a general, sentimental wish to "do good," or a genuine interest in people, or a sense of civic duty, may be of decisive importance. On the other hand, the relationship may be primarily a professional one in which the officer consciously uses interpersonal relationships to achieve well-defined professional objectives, viz., the social rehabilitation of the probationer. In the latter case, and particularly in the case of trained officers, the personal emotional needs of the officer in relation to the probationer (i.e., needs such as the need for gratitude, appreciation, obedience, rapid progress, etc., on the part of the probationer), will usually be at a minimum, and the officer will have greater freedom of conscious and deliberate action to attain specific ends. It follows also that insight and skill in consciously using a personal relationship to attain defined professional ends, ordinarily derive from training.

Probationary treatment cannot be imposed on the probationer by the probation officer, and the ideal relationship between them is therefore a co-operative one which allows of the maximum self-activity on the part of the probationer, while at the same time leaving adequate scope for the judicious exercise of the officers's func-

tion of guidance and support. The problem is to obtain the co-operation and full participation of the probationer in the process of
planning for his own social rehabilitation, while he is at the same
time susceptible to subtle guidance and direction. This clearly requires the avoidance of paternalism or dominance on the part
of the probation officer—a requirement which is particularly difficult to meet where probationary treatment takes the form of environmental manipulation or the securing of services in behalf of the
probationer. It should be noted that the quality of the relationship
required is emotional rather than intellectual. It has its foundation
in the emotional security and self-reliance engendered by a situation in which the offender is *accepted* as he is. This means that the
probation officer should be capable of avoiding an attitude or rejection or of moral condemnation—that his concern should be with
understanding, rather than judging, the probationer. It also means
that the probation officer's approach must be expressive of genuine
warmth and interest, while at the same time dispassionate and
devoid of sentimentality. The probation officer must be able to
avoid the creation of emotional barriers by his own reactions towards the probationer and, on the other hand, must be able to
inspire, in the probationer, the necessary confidence and faith in his
own (the officer's) integrity, fair-mindedness and goodwill.

The constructive utilization of the personal relationship, or
rapport, between the probation officer and the probationer for
the purposes of treatment, represents an approach which has found
significant theoretical elaboration and refinement in the contribution of psycho-analytical psychology. It also represents the dominant approach in contemporary social case work generally. It
should not be overlooked, however, that this approach, in essence, is
rooted in human experience everywhere; that it was already employed in some fashion by the pioneers of probation, as of other
fields of social work, and that—in rudimentary form—it is employed
today by many untrained workers in this and in allied fields.

It should be noted that:

> The burden of creating a friendly relationship with the pro-
> bationer falls almost entirely upon the officer. From his initial
> contact with the man committed to his care, he should strive

to make clear his own desire to be of assistance and his need for the co-operation of the probationer in what must be a mutual enterprise to re-establish the offender in society. Not infrequently the necessity of winning the probationer's confidence and support is the most difficult of all the problems of supervision. Since little of a constructive nature can be accomplished without this foundation on which to build, it often occurs that the major portion of the officer's efforts during supervision are expended in gaining the probationer's confidence. In many cases, stubborn barriers erected over a long period of years have to be broken down. Moreover fear of the officer and the prison may set up a social distance, difficult to bridge.

Points of Departure in Probationary Treatment

The unit of probationary treatment is the total personality of the probationer, seen in relationship with his social environment. Particular steps in the total process of treatment, however, will focus on particular needs of the probationer—needs which relate to certain "focal points in the life and environment of .... probationers which can be utilized as points of departure in the process of rehabilitation." Among these there are the physical and mental health, capacities, and requirements of the probationer; family relationships and home conditions; leisure and recreation; employment and economic status; education; group participation; etc. Each one of these may be changed from a handicap into a positive factor for rehabilitation. No single one, however, offers an "easy way" toward the attainment of this objective. Each of these "points of departure" in probationary treatment is, in fact, of greatest significance in the total process of the social rehabilitation of the offender only when it is skilfully utilized and brought into relationship with the total plan of treatment. Actually these "points of departure" are secondary rather than primary foci of probationary treatment—they do not relate to the dynamics of the offender's personality, but only to certain basic features of his *equipment* for social functioning (physical and mental health and capacities, and education) and to the basic elements of his social environment and group relationships (home and family, employment, leisure time activities and group relationships) . In practice, however, the efforts of probation officers are very frequently largely related to these secondary "points of departure", rather than directly and systematically concerned with the dynamics of the probationer's personality. The relative emphasis placed on the latter aspect of probationary treatment, necessarily varies with the level of professional skill attained by the probation officer.

The extent to which each of these secondary "points of departure" will require direct activity on the part of the probation officer or the probation department, also varies greatly with the nature and variety of the resources at the direct disposal of the probation department or the court (clinics, psychiatric personnel, etc.) , and with the availability of specialized service organizations in the community. In general, the probation officer will be well advised not to undertake a task which may be dealt with more effectively by other agencies in the community.

Physical and Mental Health

Effective treatment for physical and mental disorders may in some cases make a major contribution towards the social rehabilitation of an offender. Where adequate preliminary enquiries, prior to the court's disposition of a case, are carried out, medical, psychiatric and psychological data on the probationer are available to the probation officer when an offender is placed on probation. In the absence of such data, however, it is difficult to plan realistically for the probationer's social rehabilitation; under such circumstances it seems desirable that, where feasible, the administrators of probation should arrange appropriate medical, psychiatric and psychological examinations. Where possible, the probation officer should bring the probationer in contact with available community facilities for appropriate medical or psychiatric treatment.

In present-day probation practice, provision is seldom made for the adequate medical, psychiatric and psychological examination, and the appropriate treatment of probationers. Courts, on occasion, insist that appropriate medical treatment be obtained in the case of venereal or other highly infectious diseases. Similarly, it is sometimes required that probationers should submit themselves to psychiatric treatment. It will be clear, however, that the possibilities of using medical and psychiatric examination and treatment as aids in probationary treatment will be limited by the extent to which public or other free health services are available, or by the extent to which special financial provision is made for such treatment for probationers.

Family Relationships and Home Conditions

It is self-evident that the problem of an offender's social rehabilitation is ultimately connected with his family relationships and home circumstances, and that in probation due regard should therefore be given to family and home.

Close contact between the probation officer and the family of the probationer is essential, in the first instance, because it represents a prerequisite to an adequate understanding of the probationer and of the driving forces of his behavior.

In the second instance, continuing unfavourable home conditions will militate against whatever beneficial effects contacts with the probation officer may have on the probationer. It is therefore necessary that the probation officer should not only establish the facts of the home situation, but should actively engage in the task of rendering the family and home situation conducive to the offender's social rehabilitation. The least that is required is that the probation officer should co-operate with the family of the probationer. Discussion with parents, or husband or wife, as the case may be, may help to solve or clarify difficulties.

> One of his principal duties during supervision is that of harmonizing the family relationships of his charge. In many instances, he is able to do this merely by friendship, guidance and advice. Frequently he is called upon to interpret the probationer's conduct to the family, to make them see the probationer's delinquency, not as an independent act of wilfulness for which the probationer alone is responsible, but rather as the result of shortcomings and faults in the family situation.

When the family situation indicates it, it is desirable to recognize that it may be advisable to consider the family, rather than the individual probationer, as the unit of treatment.

The direct contacts between the probation officer and the family and home of the probationer also consititute a significant "op-

portunity to do effective and far-reaching preventive work," in so
far as probation supervision can be utilized also "to do rehabilitative work with those members of his (the probationer's) family
who, though not yet delinquent, are exposed to the same influences which contributed to the probationer's anti-social habits
and attitudes."

The probation officer will generally not be able to deal adequately, through his own direct efforts, with home situations
which are particularly involved and in need of specialized assistance. In such cases he will primarily rely on the services of family
welfare and related organizations in the community, and will
attempt "to arouse in the individual members [of the family] the
willingness and active desire to secure the aid they require in order
to improve the conditions of their common environment."

Employment

The employment status of an offender is very often of primary
significance for his rehabilitation. In the first instance, many offenders have long records of irregular employment or of unemployment, and are very often unskilled. In addition, offenders
frequently lose their positions through the circumstances of arrest,
detention and trial. When there is a direct relationship between an
offender's employment history (poor performance, lack of interest,
frequent dismissal or change of employment, etc.) and his offence,
the importance of obtaining suitable and satisfactory employment is even more pronounced. In the United States of
America, the *Attorney General's Survey of Release Procedures*
(1939) has found that regular employment shows the highest correlation with "success" on probation of all the factors studied and,
conversely, that lack of employment is more significantly associated
with an unfavourable outcome of release on probation than any
of the other factors studied. Assistance in finding suitable employment has accordingly been one of the oldest and most general
functions undertaken by probation officers in relation to the supervision of probationers. While the importance of suitable, regular
employment in the social rehabilitation of the probationer is widely
recognized, it is often extremely difficult to use this potential tool

with maximum effectiveness. The reason for this is twofold, namely, the special employment problems presented by probationers, on the one hand, and the inevitable limitations of the available facilities for vocational guidance, training, etc. Probationers present special employment problems as a result of the bias of employers, as a result of ineffectual work habits and lack of skill and training on the part of the probationer, as a result of unsuitability for immediate employment through long unemployment or other reasons, etc. It is therefore of particular importance that *suitable* employment should be found—employment which is capable of holding the worker's interest and of providing a sense of personal satisfaction in its achievement. For this purpose it is necessary for the probation officer to maintain close co-operation with employment exchanges and agencies offering vocational guidance and special training, where such agencies exist. It is conceivable that public employment services may employ special methods and techniques to meet the employment needs of probationers in a way similar to that in which special methods and techniques are applied to meet the needs of other categories, such as physically handicapped and older workers. It is necessary that probation authorities, in co-operating with employment services, should assist the latter in defining the special employment needs and problems of probationers, and in developing the required special methods of dealing with the problem. In larger and well-organized probation departments, it is sometimes possible to have some measure of staff specialization with reference to problems of vocational guidance and employment. Very frequently, however, the supervising officer has to take a great deal of initiative, and has to make special efforts to supplement the initiative and efforts of the probationer in relation to obtaining suitable employment.

Group Relationships and Leisure-time Activity

The social rehabilitation of an offender is primarily a matter of the modification of attitudes, and in this connection his group relationships are of decisive importance.

The attitudes of the individual are largely a product of social contacts. The contacts that are of the greatest importance in determining attitudes are those that are frequent and intimate, as in the family, the play-group, and the neighbourhood. The procedure for modifying attitudes consists essentially in changing the person's group relations. For this purpose it is necessary either to remove the probationer from the web of his former relations or insert new elements into that web of relations. While it is easier to remove the probationer from his situation, the modification of the situation is more profitable in the long run.

It should be noted that the problem of criminal behavior is also, in a certain sense, a problem of social isolation, or isolation from normal, intimate and mutually satisfactory interpersonal relationships. From this point of view, the task of probation is "to break up the social isolation" of the offender by promoting the establishment of new and constructive relationships.

As Sutherland has said, "the probation officer is limited in his capacity to become a member of the probationer's intimate groups, and consequently he must work largely through other groups." The importance of family relationships in this connection has already been discussed, and in a certain sense—namely, in so far as it is a matter of group relationships—the question of suitable employment is part of the same general problem. It is, however, necessary to go beyond the probationer's family relationships and employment, and the importance of leisure-time activities is apparent. Organized group and recreational activities (clubs, youth organizations, recreational programmes, etc.) may on occasion be utilized with considerable effect in the reorientation of the attitudes of an offender.

Education

A last principal focal point for the efforts of the probation officer relates to education and educational activities. In the case of young offenders or truants it is often a matter of great urgency to obtain their co-operation with a view to the continuation of formal schooling. Similarly, vocational training has a direct relationship to employment and economic adjustment, and is therefore of primary importance. Educational activities of a varied nature (adult classes, hobbies, etc.) may be utilized in finding ways and means of self-expression for the probationer, and in stimulating constructive interest and aspirations.

The Disciplinary Element in Probationary Treatment

Probationary supervision inevitably involves a disciplinary element. The probation officer acts on behalf of the law enforcement authorities, and of necessity has to exercise a negative or restraining influence. On behalf of the law enforcement authorities, the probation officer is obliged to keep informed with respect to the probationer's where-abouts and conduct, and to enforce the requirements imposed by the court. It is impossible to lay down any general rules with respect to the question as to how strictly the probation officer should endeavour to enforce the conditions of the probation order, and the circumstances in each individual case must determine the corresponding decision. The dangers of excessive laxity on the part of the probation officer are, however, obvious.

> When a probation order is made it is important that it should be enforced. To allow a probationer to disobey the conditions laid down in the order, and to disregard the authority of the probation officer, is to throw discredit on the system. It is clearly undesirable to take serious notice of minor lapses of conduct. For these, a personal warning. . . . may be sufficient, or the Court can take advantage of its power to impose a fine. But the ultimate sanction for disobedience to a probation order is the power of the Court to impose the punishment which might have been inflicted for the original offence, and when a probationer shows no desire whatever to respond to the opportunity given to him for reformation, he ought, after due warning, to be brought before the Court and dealt with in this way. . . . It would greatly strengthen the probation system if persons who have escaped punishment by an undertaking given as a condition of probation, are made to realize that punishment for the original offence will follow if they decline to abide by their undertaking.

The avoidance of excessive laxity in probationary supervision is equally important from the point of view of the acceptance of probation by the public. Indeed, "public support and cooperation are difficult to obtain for any probation system which does not assure the community the minimum protection of vigilance against renewed criminal activity on the part of probationers."

The importance of the disciplinary element in probationary

supervision seems to vary with the degree to which probation has come to be accepted as a method for the treatment of offenders—it is often emphasized in an attempt to make probation acceptable in communities still dominated by the punitive approach to criminal treatment. It is generally recognized, however, that the enforcement of the restrictions imposed by the court on the behavior of the probationer, is *not* the primary purpose of probationary supervision. Probationary treatment nevertheless derives an unmistakeably authoritarian character from the fact that the probation officer has the power to invoke legal sanctions against the probationer. Probationary treatment is therefore "social case work in an authoritarian setting."

The probation officer's position of authority seems to affect his relationship to the probationer differently in the case of different age groups. Adult probationers appear to be more inclined than juveniles to resent their position in relation to the probation officer, whereas a marked resistance to authority is frequently encountered in the case of adolescents or young adults. In the case of juvenile offenders, on the other hand, the probation officer's role is often a quasi-parental one, and authoritative guidance is frequently accepted readily if it is offered with tact and understanding. Moreover, it is at present realized that the use of authority may in itself be of therapeutic value, particularly in the case of juvenile anti-social personalities. It is indeed one of the principal functions of the probation officer "to epitomize and clarify authority" to the probationer. With special reference to juvenile probation, Tappan has succinctly formulated the potential positive value of the use of authority:

> Characteristically the delinquent child has suffered from an inadequate relationship to authority because of an insufficiency, an inconsistency, or an excess of controls from his surrounding environment. .... Probation case work .... must accept realistically the need for authority, indeed even emphasizes it, since it is here that the child's relation to society has been peculiarly defective.

A dominant function of the probation officer is to establish clearly in the mind of the probationer the conditions of probation, i.e., the circumstances under which society, as represented by the court, will permit him his freedom .... Without that moral condemnation which can only produce hostility, but objectively and very definitely, the worker must make the offender see that violation of the law entails certain consequences both from the state and the community in the way others will look upon him and how he must look upon himself. The alternatives should be seen by the child as the inevitable aspects of authority with which he must come to grips and from which only he can make choices. The probationer must be brought to see that he is himself the active element who must choose to conform or defy the realities that confront him.

Probation may represent to the child the first situation in which he has been accepted calmly and objectively, but warmly, for what he is as an individual—without threats or promises—and has been held to a standard of conduct imposed under definite and invariable authority: a situation in which he can choose whether to conform but must see the consequences of his deviation and must be prepared to accept them as the inevitable product of what he does. To many a child this clear focusing of authority is a new experience and it, with the clarification of his personal responsibility in the shaping of his conduct, may provide a powerful motive in his movement toward socialized adjustment.

Police and other Law Enforcement Personnel as Probation Officers

The first statute providing for the appointment of an official probation officer—the Massachusetts statute of 1878—envisaged the appointment of a suitable person "either from the police force of said city [Boston] or from the citizens at large ..," and provided that the officer should be under the general control of the chief of police. It may be said, however, that probation has altogether outgrown this early association with the law enforcement authorities, and today there exists general agreement as regards the unsuitability of police and other law enforcement officers for the purposes of exercising probationary supervision. The functions of law enforcement and probation officers, respectively, are basically different, and the association of law enforcement officers with probation work cannot fail to compromise the essential nature of probation as the non-punitive treatment of offenders, nor can it fail to create a danger that probation may, either in reality or in the public mind, become an adjunct to detection, prosecution, and punitive or disciplinary surveillance.

The Training of Probation Officers

Probationary supervision has developed from a relatively simple process in which probation officers "advise, assist and befriend" probationers, to a skilled operation on which an extensive body of theoretical knowledge is brought to bear. This distinction between benevolent assistance and skilled treatment is of great practical significance. Without the necessary training and understanding "there is a temptation to rely on temporary palliatives, such as gifts of money, or on other measures which may keep the probationer out of mischief but will not prove a permanent cure." Similarly, the finding of employment, and other auxiliary forms of assistance can only be fully utilized in the interests of the probationer's social rehabilitation if it is done with an adequate understanding of his personality needs and his likely responses. Above all, refined understanding and skill are required for the constructive utilization of the personal relationship between officer and offender.

Probationary supervision has reached a stage of development at which it has come to be exceedingly uneconomical and impractical to expect probation officers to acquire the necessary knowledge and insight and skill for their profession through trial and error—the interests of efficiency demand the systematic accumulation and transmission of experience and applied knowledge, in order that new recruits to the service may be enabled to avail themselves, to the maximum extent, of existing knowledge and experience. The question is no longer whether or not special training for probation officers is essential, but rather what are the most appropriate substance and methods of such training.

The scientific foundation of probation as a method for the treatment of offenders is to be found in the contemporary sciences of human behavior, i.e., the social, psychological and biological sciences, and in the application of these sciences to the problems of criminal behavior. The basic methods employed in probationary supervision are the methods of social case work. It is therefore essential that the training of probation officers should be based on general instruction in the behavior sciences, in the applications of these sciences to the problems of criminal behavior, and in the principles and methods of social case work. In addition the probation officer should have an adequate knowledge of community resources, and should be able to evaluate the probationer's needs in relation to such resources with a view to making appropriate referrals. Finally, he should be equipped with adequate knowledge of the law and court procedure relating to probation.

Generally speaking, it may be said that today the actual professional qualifications of probation officers fall far short of even the minimum standards which are recognized as desirable. Significant progress has been made, however, in various jurisdictions—particularly in specific jurisdictions in the United States of America and on a national scale in England and Wales.

Suggested Minimum Professional Qualifications for Probation Officers in the United States of America

Probation services in the United States of America are highly decentralized. There is therefore no national system of training of probation officers, nor any general uniformity with respect to required educational and/or professional qualifications. Several significant and authoritative attempts have been made, however, to lay down minimum standards designed to serve as a goal in the development of the personnel standards of specific probation units.

As early as 1923 a joint committee of the United States Children's Bureau and the National Probation Association proposed the following minimum educational and professional qualifications for probation personnel in juvenile courts:

(a) *Education.*— Preferably graduation from college or its equivalent, or from a school of social work.

(b) *Experience.*—At least one year in case work under supervision.

In 1938 the Department of Justice established the following educational and professional qualifications as the minimum requirements for personnel entering the federal probation service:

In view of the technical nature of the duties of probation officers, and the preparation and training necessary to fulfill adequately the requirements of such positions, the following minimum standards for the selection of probation officers are promulgated for the guidance of all concerned:

(*a*) . . . .

(*b*) They should be graduates of a college or university of recognized standing or have equivalent practical training in probation work or in an allied field. One year of study in a recognized school of social work may be substituted for two years of college training.

(*c*) They should have had at least two years full-time experience in probation work or two years full-time experience as a case worker in an accredited professional family service agency or other social case work agency, or equivalent experience in an allied field. . . .

In 1945, the National Probation Association (now the National Probation and Parole Association) published its *Standards for Selection of Probation and Parole Officers*. These *Standards* contain specific requirements with respect to educational and professional qualifications under three headings (viz., specialized knowledge, education and experience) , as follows:

Specialized Knowledge

1. The officer must have a working knowledge of the principles and practices of social case work. . . .

[This includes an understanding of individual motivation, of the relationships of physical, mental emotional health to conduct, of family problems and relationships; a knowledge of community problems and resources, including employment agencies, group work and other social and community co-operating agencies. The officer must also have the ability to keep clear and adequate records and to prepare concise reports.]

2. As an administrative agent of the court. . . . the officer must be familiar with the specific laws within which he operates, and the powers and limitations of his position. . . .

3. The officer must be familiar with the operation of related law-enforcement agencies in his jurisdiction.

Minimum Qualifications for Entering Probation . . . Work

1. *Education:* A bachelor's degree from a college or university of recognized standing, or its educational equivalent, with courses in the social sciences.

The best training for probation . . . . work is in a graduate school of social work. However, the educational requirement above is probably as much as can be required as a minimum in many parts of the country today.

For the purposes of this section social sciences include the following: sociology, psychology, anthropology, economics, political science, it being preferable that the applicant shall have a balanced program in these subjects. . . .

2. *Experience:* One year of paid full-time experience under competent supervision in an approved social agency or related field. One year in an accredited school of social work with field work practice may be substituted. If the probation . . . . department is equipped to provide in-service training under adequate supervision the requirement for previous experience may be waived.

By a related field is meant such professional work as teaching; personnel work in industry where the applicant did actual adjustment work with individuals, not merely employment service; or case work in an institution or correctional agency. When an in-service training program is provided by the department in lieu of preliminary experience, it should be an organized program of training, sustained over a period of at least one year. . . .

7

PROBATION ADDENDUM*

Probation is a humanatarian method of administering justice, not a gesture of leniency. As a substitute for imprisonment, it is in large measure a counseling service which emphasizes guidance and supportive supervision. Its objective is to develop positive social attitudes and behavior in offenders while preventing the stigma of incarceration and the breaking-up of family units. Probation is not punishment; paradoxically this seems to be the basic reason why numerous officials, the press, and a large part of the public oppose its use.

Not everyone convicted of a crime is eligible for probation. There are no real criteria for use of probation; it is a matter of grace, and not of right. Although the offense undoubtedly influences the court's decision to substitute probation for imprisonment, even co-defendants involved in the same offense are considered individually on the basis of findings revealed through pre-sentence investigations. In many states probation is impossible to obtain if the crime is "repugnant" to society; such as crimes of violence, crimes against morals, crimes against the government, or crimes carrying mandatory life or death sentences. In Illinois, the crimes of murder, incest, forcible rape, perjury and arson preclude consideration for probation.

The Federal Statute does not require that defendants make application for probation, however, several states require such formal requests. When an application by the defendant is not required, probation is left to the discretion of the court, as one of a number of possible dispositions. The Illinois Supreme Court has stated that when probation is not requested, the court has no discretion as to the extent of punishment. In such cases the indeterminate sentence fixed by statute must be imposed. Offenders have no right to probation, nor even the right to refuse its being granted them as precedented in *Cooper* v. *United States*, the Court of Appeals held that the defendant could not refuse probation. On

---

*Clyde B. Vedder, Ph.D. and Barbara A. Kay, Ph.D.

the other hand, the Court of Appeals of Alabama decided in *Persall* v. *State* that the overwhelming weight of authority is in favor of allowing the defendant to refuse probation and take his "statutory medicine." The purpose of probation is non-penal in character, therefore an offender forced to undergo probation will hardly be susceptible to the treatment opportunity if he is opposed to it.[1]

Probationers are not selected on the basis of their need for rehabilitative casework, but rather in terms of "legal" rules, and /or the judge's hunch, whim or intuition. The financial standing of the offender, or his friends' status may be the decisive factor in selection of an offender for probation. In a sense, the probationer represents the judges ability to discern who can benefit from probation consequently both success and failure of probationers indicate the courts use of the discretionary powers vested in them. Adequate presentence investigations should be reflected in the courts decisions. Experience has indicated that offenders who have been convicted of such crimes as passing bad checks, working confidence games, committing abnormal sexual offenses are the poorest risks for successful probation. However, probationers should be selected on the basis of scientific knowledge about human behavior. Many adult offenders do not require the controlled environment of a prison. They would respond well to the opportunity of operating under a restrictive program outside of an institution.

Most probation laws provide that the probation agency make a pre-sentence investigation, and prepare a report for the court, although the judge is not bound by law to consider the report. The use of pre-sentence investigation reports and recommendations for or against the use of probation as a part of the court process raises some serious issues concerning "due process." For example, must the court permit the defendant to view the report, to cross examine the probation officer, or to offer evidence on his own behalf? Constitutional right to due process of law is violated when the above are not available to those seeking probation[2]. Nevertheless, some courts rely upon questionable recommendations of underpaid, politically appointed, untrained probation officers who con-

---

1 Arne R. Johnson: Recent Developments in the Law of Probation. *The Journal of Criminal Law, Criminology and Police Science*, 53:201, June, 1962.
2 *Ibid.*, p. 195.

duct inadequate pre-sentence investigations and interject their personal biases into their reports.

One of the most vexing problems of efficacy concerning probation are the "conditions" of probation. Many stipulations of probation are unrealistic, difficult to enforce, impossible to abide by, and serve no purpose if observed. In most jurisdictions the statutory conditions of probation are neither mandatory nor all-inclusive. The Federal Statute states that certain conditions are among those that the defendant may be required to observe. In some states all statutory conditions are imposed upon each offender in addition to non-statutory stipulations conjured up under the guise of justice by the court. A condition of probation should not be illegal, immoral or impossible of performance or enforcement. Many offenders fail on probation, not because they commit a new offense, but rather because they have violated the unrealistic and often non-functional "conditions" of probation.

Probation may be handicapped by attempting to apply two rather divergent goals simultaneously. (1) Social casework although difficult to implement in an authoritarian setting must be the method of treatment made available to the probationer. (2) Pre-sentence investigations to aid in the selection of those who can benefit most from non-institutional treatment and the supervisory process to protect society from further depredations of the offender comprise the complex of purposive responsibilities assigned to probation officers. It is surprising that we have as many successes on probation as we do. The probationer may accept probation as the lesser of two evils. Many probation officers are not familiar with social casework philosophy and resort to "ordering and forbidding" techniques. The image of probation is blurred by inconsistent standards, organizational and administrative differences within the states, between the states, as well as between the states and the federal government. No state has a really state-wide probation system with trained men and women competent to handle presentence investigations and supervision.

The competent probation officer is neither a strong-arm law enforcement officer nor an overly sympathetic person who relies upon promises and personal loyalty of the person under his care. Insight, patience, and a sense of practical reality are necessary in order to deal effectively with the array of problems which affect the social adjustment of probationers. It is because of the great scope of problems handled by probation services, and the diversity of knowledge needed to resolve them that many probation agencies require the probation officer applicant to possess a bachelors degree with concentration of study in the behavioral sciences, perferably sociology, criminology or psychology. Applicants for the position of "Chief Probation Officer" should be required to hold a Masters degree in Social Casework in order to properly supervise officers in their work with probationers.

Despite the difficulties inherent in probation services, the authors are convinced that use of probation should be extended. Donald Clemmer's prediction, made in his address before the Washington Chapter of the National Association of Social Workers (May 1962), that penitentiaries will be needed only for "professional mobsters" and "syndicate gangster-type hoodlums" by 1980, is a goal worth considering. Clemmer noted that the nation's crime problem is "primarily a problem of theft" and that the behavior of such offenders can be redirected. For "conventional thieves" he said we need a system of small "therapeutically-oriented institutions." Clemmer believes that a substantial increase in the use of probation services for such offenders is appropriate to overall goals and successful outcome of correctional systems.

The laws of probation have been developed considerably in the last three decades, and in the process of development a number of problems have emerged. Usually probation is granted only after conviction. Massachusetts, Rhode Island and Kentucky have granted probation prior to conviction, this is commendable because there is no "stigma of conviction," the probationer does not loose his civil rights, and it provides a greater stimulus "to make good."

The Federal Probation Service is closest to the broad purposes of correctional philosophy. The federal approach of granting the defendant a hearing when revocation occurs might well be used as a model for the states. Certainly some minimum "due process of law" should be concommitent to probation. The defendant's rights can be best served by statutory and not by constitutional restrictions. In order to have an effective probation system, the hands of the

sentencing judge should not be tied. The federal rule denying the
defendant the right to refuse probation should be over-ruled.
Similarly, the rule that only the sentencing judge can revoke probation should be abandoned. State distinctions between suspension of imposition and suspension of execution of sentence are
highly undesireable. The Ohio practice of placing no time limit on
duration of probation should not be encouraged elsewhere. The
legislatures should redefine the offenses for which probation is
available according to some rational schema. Conflicting laws based
on percedented cases concerning restitution, etc. as a condition of
probation need clarification. We should capitalize upon the assets
and rid ourselves of the deficiencies in the laws of probation[3].

Probation is an enlightened attempt to cope with a crisis in the
life of an offender who possesses rehabilitative potential. It is often
misunderstood and underrated by the public because the press
coverage is so frequently negative. Probation is less dramatic than
incarceration, and neither probation officers nor successful probationers make "good copy." Ideally, probation services are dignified.
Probation is social casework with the power of the law behind it. It
is the only really promising rehabilitative technique for violators
of the law.

3   *Ibid.,* pp. 201–202.
4   *Ibid.,* pp. 205–206.

PART II
PAROLE

8

PRINCIPLES OF PAROLE*

Generally speaking, parole is defined as the conditional release of a selected convicted person before completion of the term of imprisonment to which he has been sentenced. It implies that the person in question continues in the custody of the State or its agent and that he may be reincarcerated in the event of misbehavior. It is a penological measure designed to facilitate the transition of the offender from the highly controlled life of the penal institution to the freedom of community living. It is not intended as a gesture of leniency or forgiveness.

Under parole, there may be only a single condition imposed, namely, that the offender must refrain from committing a new offence, or there may also be—and this is more usual—several specific conditions requiring the individual to comply with a number of obligations or prohibitions. Parole conditions have the dual objectives of ensuring public safety and contributing to the rehabilitation of the individual.

The use of individualized conditions of release as well as the factor of selectivity for parole must rest upon a social study. It is the basis for parole decisions.

Parole also implies a particular kind of supervision involving guidance and assistance which sets it apart from typical police functions.

While, technically, parole may be granted without any provision for supervision, it is increasingly being accepted that supervision is a *sine qua non* and that, in fact, conditional release without supervision should not be known as parole.

Parole is to be distinguished from probation in that the latter is granted by the court as an alternative to incarceration.[1] Parole is

*Parole and Aftercare. United Nations, Dept. of Social Affairs, St/50A/SD/4, July, New York, 1954, pp. 1–9.

[1]In some legal systems the term "probation" is used in reference to the measure identified in this report as parole. For clarity, this report employs only the term

also to be distinguished from pardon, which is an act of forgiveness and remission of punishment, freeing the individual from responsibility to the State with respect to the remainder of his sentence.

CONCEPTIONS OF PAROLE

The status of parole today is still disputed. It is, on the one hand, considered as an act of clemency, the granting of which depends entirely on the prisoner's conduct in the penal institution and on his repentance. If parole were thus viewed as a favour, it would be used only in exceptional cases.

In contrast to this point of view, parole is often conceived as a penological measure in harmony with the original sentence and even, in fact, an extension of it. The individual is required to demonstrate in society his capacity to conform to the behavior standards set by the community or be returned to the institution for further training. Such a conception of parole is closely associated both with a graduated or "progressive" penal system and with the indeterminate sentence, under which the individual demonstrates his capacity to adjust through a series of stages of greater freedom, and is then released whenever the authorities believe he is capable of adjusting satisfactorily outside the institution.

Parole is also regarded as a social defence measure. From this point of view, its importance lies especially in the fact that it offers the possibility of intervening at once in cases where further criminal behavior appears imminent. In contrast to the two previous conceptions of parole, in which the more favorable cases are given primary attention, the focus here is on those individuals who are least likely to adjust successfully in freedom. This conception also rests on a system of indeterminate sentencing, although it is applied from a point of view opposite to the one referred to above. Particularly in the absence of institutions for habitual offenders and criminal psychopaths, parole as a social defence measure is seen as

---

"parole," even when referring to countries where programmes of conditioned release from imprisonment are known as probation.

Moreover, in some legal systems, measures of supervision in freedom applied by the court in lieu of incarceration are known as "bench parole." Such measures are identified in this report only by the designation probation.

providing protection to the public from a number of socially dangerous persons.

Finally, parole is conceived as the logical transitional measure applicable in principle to all offenders. Parole, in this instance, is granted in relation to the plans made by and for the individual with respect to his release and takes into consideration not only institutional adjustment but also his personality and the potential danger he constitutes to society. Eligibility is determined on the basis of a social study embracing the individual's history, activities in prison, personality and possibilities upon release. From these data are derived the conditions to be imposed as well as the nature and extent of supervision.

It is this last conception which has gained widest support today in penological circles. General public opinion, however, tends to conceive of parole as an act of clemency, and among prisoners parole is often regarded unfavourably as a social defence measure.

JUSTIFICATION FOR PAROLE

The granting of parole may limit the effects of imprisonment, which are deleterious to the offenders and ultimately to his family as well, by providing an acceptable means of shortening the period of incarceration.

There is general agreement today that no country should intentionally expose its prisoners to penalties which would seriously threaten their physical and mental health. Opinion, however, still differs on the question whether imprisonment, being a penalty, should serve as such only by the deprivation of liberty, or whether it should entail a disagreeable manner of execution, in order to emphasize its penal character. It is nevertheless agreed that it is desirable that no discharged prisoner should leave the penal institution damaged by his experiences there; but, on the contrary, that the institution should have contributed to the reformation of the prisoner during his stay.

Even when organized in accordance with such views, a prison community inevitably breeds unfavorable conditions which have a harmful influence on a number of prisoners.

The conclusion is that society is obliged at least to minimize the impact of the process of deterioration produced by imprisonment.

The consequences of the prolonged imprisonment of husband, father and/or chief supporter of a family constitute an equally urgent problem. Such imprisonment may frustrate any possibility for the social and moral reintegration of a family facing the danger of permanent breakdown. Since many imponderable factors are involved in this process, even completely adequate material support given to dependents can only partially alleviate the situation.

Parole offers an opportunity for the practical application of rehabilitation programmes prior to the expiration of sentence. Any prisoner is, to a greater or lesser degree, molded by rules and standards which are enforced either by the management of the penitentiary or by the prisoners themselves, but which prevail in an unnatural community, bearing only a superficial resemblance to free society. Modern penitentiary systems usually aim at confronting prisoners with norms that obtain in the world outside the prison walls, norms which some of the inmates had not known before or, at least, had not observed. Such efforts often have only a correspondingly superficial impact.

Upon return to society, the individual finds himself in a position to decide on his course, facing a much wider variety of modes of behavior than the institution could offer him. Parole supervision including the conditions of release which have been established, but especially the social case work involved in parole, assist the individual in making a realistic application in daily life of the behavior standards advocated in the institution. Return to the institution may follow failure to observe these standards.

The prospect of parole encourages the prisoner to maintain maximum contact with the world outside the institution. Communication with the outside world, although limited, means much more to the prison inmate than is commonly assumed. In a modern penitentiary system a variety of means of communication is employed to maintain the necessary contact. Most important to the prisoner are those which give an opportunity to maintain contact with relatives and closest friends, notably visits and correspondence. Next in importance are the meetings with other persons who come to see the prisoner, as, for example, members of a prisoner's aid society or an after-care agency, scientific investigators staying temporarily in the institution on a research job, etc.

Also important, though to a lesser degree than personal contacts, are those means of communication which keep the prisoner informed of events in the outer world, i.e., newspapers, magazines and radio. To this should be added the various means of entertainment such as films, music, stage performances and lectures.

To the prisoner all those modes of contact have a certain emotional value, since they keep him keenly aware of the existence of a free society of which he continues to be a member in spite of his incarceration.

It is understandable that the preclusion of the possibility of being paroled reduces considerably the significance to the prisoner of the contacts and communications mentioned above. In cases, although they are useful, because they render the prisoner's isolation a little less unbearable to him, the prisoner knows that, by simply serving his time, he automatically will be discharged on a specified date, irrespective of the way in which he responds to the institutional programme. Thus contacts with the world outside the prison gain greater importance when the prisoner associates them with the possibility of being granted parole.

The prospect of parole stimulates the prisoner to derive maximum benefit from the facilities provided by the prison as preparation for parole. The individual prisoner may have available to him a variety of educational, vocational, religious, recreational or other services to which he will respond with apathy or enthusiasm, depending upon his general outlook. The individual who has the prospect of parole before him is more inclined to apply himself, consciously or unconsciously, to the utilization of such services.

Parole offers assistance to the individual upon release from prison. Through the supervising agent, the parolee may receive both material and psychological assistance. It is not unlikely that the assistance received, especially the advice and support given by the parole officer, may be a key factor in the successful post-institutional adjustment of many individuals.

The possibility of parole revocation acts as a deterrent. The merits of this conception of parole are presently in dispute. Although it is possible, even probable, that coercion may contribute to making parole a success, since it is unlikely that any man could be wholly indifferent to the risk of being sent back to prison, it is questionable whether the existence and application of coercive measures are in keeping with accepted principles of parole practice. It is agreed, however, that parole and after-care, as understood today, do not primarily derive their importance from the threat of possible parole revocation.

The possibility of parole may be an incentive to good conduct in the penitentiary. Undoubtedly the possibility of being paroled induces many prisoners to conform to prison regulations. It is known, however, that good conduct in prison often results from a superficial, sometimes simulated adjustment to prison rules, and is consequently of relatively little value to the person after release. Indeed, there is reason to believe that a less smooth adjustment may give evidence of the existence of a well-integrated personality. In any case, it is agreed that good conduct should not be the decisive factor for granting parole.

Parole provides a means whereby the prison term may be shortened. On the basis of observations made on the prisoner in the institution as well as other factors having to do with his social adjustment, it may be concluded that no purpose is served, either to the individual or to society by his continued incarceration. While unconditional release would be unwarranted from the standpoint of social protection, the granting of parole, allowing for immediate return to prison if necessary, as well as supervision and assistance, would meet both the humanitarian and the penological objectives in shortening the original sentence.

Parole allows the timing of release to be related to the completion of vocational and other training programmes. Frequently, prison officials encounter the difficult problem of preventing the deterioration of prisoners who, having undergone complete vocational training in the institution, are not given the opportunity to use their newly gained abilities for long periods of time thereafter because of continued incarceration. Flexible release procedures associated with long-range parole planning enable the authorities to release the individual at the optimal time as concerns the skills he has acquired and his readiness to readjust to society.

Parole offers an opportunity for the prison administration to evalute the influences of the penal system. Before the introduction of conditional release and parole there was very little possibility of carrying out large-scale investigations into the effect of detention upon the prisoner. Parole, with its after-care contacts, has made extensive and thorough explorations in this field feasible, because the parole agencies are designed to maintain close contact with the parolee and to watch his career for a period of time. Clearly, this situation offers an opportunity to gain an understanding of the extent to which the penal institution contributes to socially satisfactory behavior in freedom, and, on the other hand, to determine whether inappropriate or insufficient prison treatment should be held responsible for post-institutional failures.

Parole is socially just in that it enables society to play an auxiliary role in the readjustment of the individual who became a criminal partly through shortcomings in society itself. Certain existing social conditions, it is agreed, are determining factors of crime. Accordingly, the support that society may give to a discharged offender implies, in a certain sense, a concept of mutual responsibility.

Parole may serve as a means for mitigating excessively severe punishments inflicted under the influence of aroused public emotions. The extent to which popular indignation will influence the course and outcome of a trial is closely connected with the organization of criminal jurisdiction in the country concerned and it is therefore quite variable. Although most legislation provides for special procedures, such as pardon, to rectify a gross injustice, such provisions are not generally applied in cases where it is exclusively a question of unduly severe sentences. On the other hand, it is generally agreed that this is an improper use of parole, and that parole should be used exclusively as a social transitional measure and not to correct injustices, for which other measures should be applied.

Parole offers a means of protection to society from further criminal activity on the part of released offenders. Parole supervision and the power to return the individual to prison provide safeguards to the public during the critical period following the release from imprisonment. The safeguards, on the other hand, operate as potent influences on the individual during the readjustment period. It is generally held that the fact that parole implies a certain risk for society should not be considered as a valid reason against it, in as much as there are ethical grounds for taking a certain degree of risk if it is assumed that society itself has a partial responsibility for the causation of crime.

Parole offers the opportunity to re-evaluate the role of institutional treatment and the relative merits of alternatives. Parole, along with the companion service of probation, has demonstrated the efficacy of non-institutional treatment of offenders. These measures have led to a shift in emphasis, including increased skepticism regarding the merits of imprisonment and greater reliance on non-punitive techniques.

PREPARATION FOR PAROLE

Many modern penitentiary systems have adopted the principle that the entire penitentiary treatment should from the outset be directed towards parole, in the hope that it may be granted to every prisoner. This principle can be given effect only if imprisonment in its entirety is viewed as preparation for liberty.

This conception is fundamental for the application of various treatment methods usually referred to as social education, re-education, correctional education, etc. At the same time, it embodies the cardinal principle of modern penitentiary administration, namely, that the aim of penitentiary treatment is success in the future rather than revenge for the past.

"Education" may have a variety of meanings. In its wider sense education may be applied to the life experiences of any person having potentiality for maturation. Although it may be held that many prison inmates are juvenile or immature as concerns their personality structure, there is no justification for the use of educational methods designed for children. Among children immaturity is but a part of the normal growth process; immaturity in adults borders on the pathological.

Programmes for the re-education of prisoners must be based on a recognition of the specialized nature of the educational objectives to be achieved.

To this end, provision must be made for:

1. Expert clinical observation of the prisoner;
2. Individual treatment from the outset, based on the results

of the results of the observation (so-called "progressive" reg-
imens where all prisoners regularly are promoted from class
to class would not be suitable) ;
3. Flexibility of general regulations, which should be adaptable
as far as possible to the circumstances of every individual
prisoner.

In many penal systems parole has been designed as the last phase
of a series of phases separated from each other within what is called
a "progressive system."

In a system, however, as referred to above, which is progressive
without being a "progressive system" in the strict sense, such a
sequence of phases does not exist, and there would not be a clear-cut
special "parole preparation" phase, even though, during the last
months of incarceration, problems with regard to the impending
parole would receive special attention.

Generally it is very doubtful if a short "parole preparation"
phase is of value unless it is associated with a regimen that is consistently rehabilitative. This applies especially to antiquated systems which serve only security purposes and in which the concept
of parole seems to be out of place. In such systems it is doubtful if
a short preparation for conditional release would be sufficient to
bridge the gap between imprisonment and freedom. In any case, the
process of preparing the prisoner for parole is time-consuming and
cannot be compressed into a brief period immediately preceding release on parole.

Today, efficient examination with regard to parolability has so
many scientific aspects that it is impossible to entrust it to one expert. In addition to thorough psychiatric training, profound knowledge of social relations in general is necessary. Ample knowledge in
the penological and criminological field is equally needed. The conclusion is that only teamwork by experts in the various fields provides the solution.

Irrespective of the authority by which the decision regarding
the granting or denying of parole is ultimately to be taken, the entire parole examination may be carried out by prison officials.

In such circumstances, the entire examination is carried out by the prison staff not only of the personality but also of his social life outside the prison. These particulars may be assembled not only by questionnaire but also by personal research made by investigating prison officials.

Various objections have been raised against this method of parole examination. To the prisoner the prison staff is generally identified as being in opposition and therefore he may be inclined in advance to have doubt as to the objectivity of the examination. If the examination into outside social aspects is to be carried out by a social assistant attached to the prison staff, but working outside the prison, the prisoner may still have doubts on the ground that the assistant will be too much influenced by the opinion of the staff. The main objection, however, is based on the claim that officials working in a prison are subject themselves to prison influences, which incline them to view matters preponderantly from an unduly cautious, negative or punitive point of view.

Personnel not affiliated with the prison administration, although working in behalf of the prison, are generally not subject to this charge. They are regarded as being more impartial and frequently find it easier to gain the confidence of the prisoners than do prison officials. It is extremely difficult, however, to find officers capable of carrying out parole examinations both within the prison and outside. The non-institutional official may often lack the psychological insight and the skill to evaulate institutional adjustments which his prison colleague possesses. Nevertheless, the independent position of such officials vis-a-vis prison authorities is held to be an important advantage.

Sometimes pre-release studies are carried out by specialists connected with a private agency, working exclusively or partially in the field of parole supervision. This may be the case especially in countries in which parole supervision and after-care are entrusted to non-governmental agencies. Such agencies, strongly motivated towards aiding prisoners, are in danger of placing insufficient stress on the aspects of social protection to the community.

Sometimes laymen, generally volunteer members of after-care agencies, may make the investigation. This has all the disadvantages referred to above in connection with the specialist, plus the factor of lack of expert knowledge.

On the other hand, the inquiries may be carried out by professional personnel acting on behalf of the official parole-granting authority working in close co-operation with prison administration authorities as well as with the after-care agencies. This system offers great advantages. It prevents one-sidedness, whether on the part of prison officials or on the part of agency personnel, because both the co-ordination of the data and the formulation of the advice are undertaken by specialists holding neither the institutional nor the after-care agency's special points of emphasis.

CONTENT OF PAROLE EXAMINATION

If no social history data are available because they were not obtained either during the pre-sentence period or earlier during the prison period, they should be collected as the time for the parole decision approaches. Occasionally this is a difficult task. It may require establishing contact with persons who had known the prisoner previously and it may mean corresponding with other prisons, etc. In some cases, very little outside information can be obtained at all. Along with such data, observations on the individual's behaviour and personality in the prison should be made.

In a modern prison system, observations and study should be carried on throughout the entire period of imprisonment, although intensity and emphasis may shift during the period.

In general, incarceration should begin with a period of close observation, during which time decisions should be made as to the prisoner's programme in the institution and even as to the type of institution to which the individual should be sent, in those prison systems which provide diversified institutions. Subsequent observations during the general period of imprisonment will supplement the original observations.

If thorough observation has been made throughout the period of incarceration, special pre-parole examinations will probably not be necessary, although a special inquiry during the final phases may still be required.

Until recently, personality examination often has been viewed as a responsibility exclusively of psychologists and psychiatrists. Without underestimating the role of these specialists, it has been found advisable to supplement their clinical examinations with data obtained from prison officers, even from those of the lowest rank, who are, after all, in closest contact with the prisoners.

The task of the psychologist or psychiatrist will be facilitated by the help of a trained social worker, who should report on the social background of the prisoner. Although it might be claimed that for personality examination *stricto sensu* it might be sufficient to rely only on the prisoner's version, it is advisable to have an objective picture of the background which can be compared with the prisoner's interpretation.

For parole purposes, information on environmental changes which have taken place during the prisoner's incarceration is important. These changes may refer, *inter alia,* to new family situations resulting from the absences of the prisoner who was the main support. Even if the wife has taken over this role and has prevented family disintegration, new situations are to be expected. These and other possible changes create situations that the parolee will meet and for which he should be prepared.

Another important aspect to be considered is the reaction of the community to the prisoner as a result of the offense committed. This is particularly important when the parolee will be returning to a small community.

The importance of vocational skills and experience is generally accepted, but not infrequently this importance has been overestimated. Such overestimation has occasionally led to the erroneous conclusion that parole and after-care are synonymous with the procuring of employment.

As regards vocational background, it is particularly advisable that a thorough pre-sentence examination should provide information regarding the vocational activities and capacities of the prisoner. If these data are not available, it may be extremely difficult to reconstruct the vocational background of a prisoner on the basis of the data he provides. Very often, and for a variety of understandable reasons, the information given by prisoners cannot be accepted as altogether reliable.

All data thus far discussed contribute to answering these important questions: When and under what conditions is parole justified? Is it to be expected that the prisoner will become involved in crime again?

The answers are not easy and for years criminologists have been experimenting with methods to facilitate the accuracy of prediction of parole success or failure. In the U. S. A. research in this matter has led to the composition of prediction tables as instruments for estimating parolability. Opinions differ as to the elements to be considered in the preparation of such tables; some writers stress the importance of factors constituting the basic pattern of personality during the early years of childhood; others express the opinion that this is too static a concept and place more emphasis on the intricate interrelations between individual development and environmental influences. Still other writers stress the important influence exercised upon prisoners by their penitentiary surroundings or that of biological and hereditary factors which are evaluated in very different ways.

ROLE OF THE JUDICIARY IN GRANTING AND REVOKING PAROLE

Although the participation of the judiciary in the granting of parole has been advocated in some quarters, such participation may involve serious practical difficulties. For example, it is extremely difficult for a judge to evaluate after a lapse of years, even having at his disposal the adequate information, whether or not and when parole should be granted. The most serious objection, however, is that such decision is outside of the judicial function which is ordinarily limited to the determination of guilt and the passing of sentence. In some countries, however, the judge's views may be sought by the paroling authority as to granting parole but the merit of even this limited intervention has been challenged.

With respect to the revocation of parole, two different aspects should be considered: a) revocation because the parolee committed a new offence and b) revocation by infringement of the conditions imposed on the parolee. With respect to a) the judicial intervention is called for in connection with the new offence; as for b) although the decision can be left to the parole authority, it is sometimes found useful to have some form of judicial intervention in case the parolee lodges an appeal against the parole authority. More-over, it is often advocated that the participation of the judiciary is warranted to assure that no injustice may be done and even to advise on certain questions of rights and equity occasionally involved. This intervention is handled in a variety of ways, foremost among which is the setting up of a board in which the judiciary participates.

From another point of view, the participation of the judiciary is advocated as a source of stimulation toward a deeper concern for and a greater insight into the total problem of the treatment of offenders.

9

PRINCIPLES OF AFTER-CARE*

NATURE AND SCOPE OF AFTER-CARE

AFTER-CARE FOR OFFENDERS originated in the relief work for discharged prisoners. The possibility of parole changed the favour of aid and support, which could be bestowed upon a discharged prisoner, into a necessity, which had to be organized. Although in the beginning conditional release was designed primarily as a measure to hold the released prisoner under control, it is clear that the development of conditional release under control into parole under supervision and with after-care was inevitable.

In marked contrast to the past, the principle of trust has gained a very important place in the policy of modern penal administration. Nevertheless in the penal institution the trust-margin cannot be very extensive. The application of this principle is, accordingly, very limited and the prison community seldom loses the character of an enforced community of prisoners and guards.

This situation changes considerably as soon as the parolee enters free society. The granting of parole is, in fact, already an act of trust. It is possible to build on to the trust already established during incarceration, and to continue this policy during the parole period. The core of the relationship between parolee and parole supervisor becomes the slow and careful extension of this trust in forms adapted to the personality of the parolee.

If, however, the essential element of the supervision is control, the relationship takes on the character of police surveillance. Sometimes, parole supervisors may even be invested with powers which normally only are executed by the police as, for example, the power to arrest the parolee in case of breach of the rules. Such forms of supervision are probably of very little positive value as far as the parolee is concerned although they give the public the illusion of maximum protection.

However, trusting supervision also has its dangers, especially if

---

*Parole and Aftercare, United Nations, Dept. of Social Affairs, ST/50A/SD/4, New York, July 1954, pp. 10-15.

the supervisor fails to limit the trust given to that quantity of trust the parolee can handle wisely. Yet, there can be no doubt that, as contrasted with the sterile atmosphere of supervision with a wholly or preponderating controlling character, trusting supervision offers the opportunity for fruitful after-care work.

If parole were merely conditional release without after-care, one should always have to be restricted to those prisoners who might be able to get along without supervision, i.e., to the so-called "good risks." This, however, would mean that the very men who had lapsed into criminality because they needed care and did not get it, should never be paroled, which would not only be unjust, but dangerous as well.

It is, thus, understandable as well as justifiable that with the development of after-care, parole has been extended also to prisoners not belonging to the "best risks" category. In former times, eligibility for parole was very limited. Often, also, parole-granting authorities were afraid to accept a certain amount of risk, overlooking the fact that risks are inevitably much more serious if the weak prisoner afterwards has to be released without parole and after-care, and yet be exposed to the same unfavourable influence. Often, agencies stressed too much the showing of favourable statistics.

THE ORGANIZATION OF AFTER-CARE

There are strong arguments presented against having parole supervision carried out by prison officials, even when specialists are available on the prison staff.

Diversification of institutions has resulted in there being in any one institution individuals from widely separate localities. Since the great majority of prisoners return to their own locality upon release, the number remaining in the vicinity of the prison will be small. Supervision by the prison staff of any released prisoners other than this small group is administratively very difficult, if not impossible.

Another objection is that it is doubtful whether the prison official is able to have as deep an insight into the difficulties and potentialities existing for the parolee in free society, as may be possessed by a parole supervisor who himself is living in the same or a similar community.

There is also the possibility of having a system, wherein

the ultimate responsibility for after-care rests with the prison staff, making use, however, of the co-operation of private agencies or other outside specialists in the after-care field. The danger that after-care matters will be viewed too heavily from the institutional point of view is not eliminated. Major decisions will be made by prison officials and these decisions will inevitably be influenced by the official's institutional orientation. Moreover, there remains the difficulty, that in the case of parolees living far from the penitentiary, the real responsibility will rest with the after-care agencies, which will not always be prepared to accept supervision from a prison official whom they may know only by name.

After-care, organized by a public agency, exclusively working in this field, has many advantages. The close administrative relationship, for example, which results from having parole handled as a government activity along with the institutions will contribute to harmony and efficiency. It gives, moreover, strong official recognition to the fact that parole and after-care are important parts of the total penal process. Especially where there are no after-care programmes created spontaneously under private auspices, governmental agencies can lead the way in establishing adequate services.

However, where private agencies do exist, even when supported and supervised by public agencies, there is often a strong public sentiment against having these services taken over by the government. Although this sentiment may be based on unwarranted scepticism of government administration, it creates a very difficult atmosphere in which to work effectively. In practice, private agencies as a rule cherish their independence and only reluctantly accept financial support from public sources, fearing they may lose in this way part of this independence.

Private agencies which receive public financial support as well as technical assistance and direction from specialists in the governmental service have been able to handle after-care responsibilities effectively while at the same time avoiding the criticism leveled either at the exclusively private or exclusively public agency.

THE CONTENT OF AFTER-CARE

An important point with regard to the transition from a penitentiary regime to after-care is the necessity to discuss with the parolee a series of important topics before he goes on parole. Primary attention must be given to the conditions of release. It is essential that they be thoroughly understood. Similar attention can profitably be given to family relationship, employment prospects, etc.

It is generally desirable that these discussions be conducted by a member of the after-care service, preferably the person who will be responsible for the supervision.

The immediately needed material provisions consist of: employment, lodgings and clothing. Of course, in every parole plan employment takes a central place. Job finding has to be based as far as possible on the outcome of parole examination with regard to labour capacities. Sometimes, employment is a prerequisite to the granting of parole. In times of prosperity it generally will be possible to find a job for the parolee—provided he has certain minimum capacities—but when economic crises and unemployment prevail, the possibilities in this field become very limited. Securing jobs for these people also may be extremely difficult because they are not available for preliminary contact with potential employers.

As a rule, it does not seem desirable to obtain employment indiscriminately simply to satisfy the condition. Particularly when the parolee has received special trade training in the institution he should have ample opportunity to seek a job most suitable to his capabilities and interests.

All parole preparation should be carried on with as active participation of the prisoner as possible. The responsibility which the individual assumes toward preparing for his release is, in fact, as important as the plans themselves.

The core of parole and after-care is the personal contact of the parolee with his parole supervisor. It is undesirable to establish fixed regulations as to the frequency of the contacts between parolee and parole supervisor. Regular contacts at fixed times and places always run the risk of degenerating into a meaningless routine. The parole supervisor must be allowed a flexibility in deciding, when, where and how often he needs to meet his parolee.

Related to this is the important principle that the parolee should always have the opportunity to reach his supervisor when necessary.

The attitude of the supervisor has to be based on the conviction that his role is to assist the parolee to obtain and maintain self-reliance. He may guide and assist but he must not substitute himself for the parolee's own initiative.

It is necessary for the sake of a sound relationship that the supervisor does not have any association with the parolee other than that of supervisor. The combination supervisor-employer has seldom been successful. Special problems also arise when supervisory powers are given to persons who already have with the parolee certain professional relationships, such as those of the clergyman or physician. Similar problems have arisen when supervisory responsibilities have been given to members of the parolee's family.

As concerns contact with the family of the parolee, the supervisor must exercise caution lest he interfere with the unity of the family. Sometimes, however, on one or both sides, such a lack of comprehension and co-operation is being displayed that his intervention is unavoidable. Also very often, the interests of the parolee and those of the family are so intermingled, that it is virtually impossible for the supervisor, discussing his parolee's problems, not to enter into the area of his family life. If the supervisor inspires confidence by his tact and understanding, he may render notable service as a counsellor in family difficulties.

It is very dangerous for the supervisor to bring in the family as an aid in controlling the parolee, without the latter's knowledge. Such arrangement may ultimately destroy both parolee-supervisor and parolee-family relationships.

In addition to assisting the individual to obtain employment the supervisor can serve effectively as a vocational counsellor to the parolee. Contact of the supervisor with the parolee's employer will be advisable only when the latter knows that his employee is on parole. These contacts have to be as limited as possible. After-care agencies in general find they have a role to play in removing prejudices and discrimination against former prisoners as concerns employment.

Within the framework of good after-care, the religious aspects of life may have considerable importance, especially for those parolees who maintain an active affiliation with some denomination. In some countries the after-care work is organized on the denominational base, but in others, where this is not the case, the religious needs of the parolee are not to be overlooked. If possible, the chaplain of the penitentiary should participate in parole preparation in collaboration with his colleagues from outside. Thereby the parole supervisor can refrain from interfering in religious matters.

In the past, financial assistance was the chief contribution of after-care agencies to released offenders. Today there is a tendency to limit this kind of material aid as much as possible. This has come about through the realization that extensive financial aid has only a superficial influence on the difficulties of the parolee whose situation is now seen to involve more complex considerations of human relations.

Inherent in the concept of control is the notion of authority, coercion and power. On the other hand after-care counselling gradually has become (especially after the introduction of case work methods) a relation on the basis of human equality, within which authority fundamentally has no place. Practical experience indicates that it is possible to imbue after-care for parolees with important elements adopted from social case work, by which the standards of after-care have been raised considerably. It is to be expected that in due time equilibrium will result, serving at the same time the interests of the parolee and those of society.

While after-care organizations must naturally maintain appropriate professional relationship with the police, no functions of supervision can be suitably delegated to them. *Inter alia*, the defined function of the police and the general attitude of released offenders to the police make such a practice unwise.

THE TERMINATION OF AFTER-CARE

In most countries prisoners are placed on parole for a specified period, often equal to the period during which they still would have been detained if they had not received parole. In the case of prisoners serving long terms, the parole period may amount to several years, especially in those countries where the granting of parole is made possible by law after one third of the sentence has been served.

The basic question is whether there should be a parole period, at all.

Although there appears to be merit in having a parole period fixed, at least tentatively, it has been demonstrated that certain individuals would benefit from having their period shortened in the course of parole whereas there is equally strong argument that certain individuals should have the parole period extended.

While it is ordinarily the case that recidivism will result in parole termination, this is not necessarily true nor advisable. If, on the basis of the offence and on the basis of the individual, there is adequate reason to believe that the parolee could achieve success if allowed to remain at liberty, the parole may be continued.

Much more and delicate than revocation as a consequence of relapse into new criminality is revocation when no offences are committed, or even when no formal transgression of rules has taken place although the social behaviour of the parolee has become so questionable as to permit serious doubts regarding his readjustment. Clearly, the utmost caution is necessary before revocation is ordered on such grounds. Here the evidence of an offence committed (and proved or confessed) is lacking. Decisions on these cases urgently call for expert knowledge in the field of parole supervision. The decisions to be reached by the parole-revoking authority should rely heavily on the information and advice of the after-care supervision.

SPECIALIZED AFTER-CARE

It is inevitable that many offenders who enter prison are more or less mentally disturbed, and even that unrecognized psychotics now and then are to be found in prisons. In some countries, it is made possible by law to detain mentally disturbed, but not insane, prisoners in special institutions. In others, special wings in existing penitentiaries are being utilized. From the after-care point of view, the mental cases require expert care to be given only by psychiatric social workers, guided by able forensic psychiatrists.

Experts generally agree that at the roots of sexual delinquency very often mental disturbances are to be found and now and then they are of a very dangerous nature. Specialized after-care for these parolees is indispensable because many sexual delinquents by their deviations gradually have become misfits in the normal world. For them it is very difficult to adapt themselves in such a way that re-

lapse into new criminality may be avoided. These people may benefit considerably by expert psychiatric treatment, aiming at readapta-
tion and social reintegration, though the sexual pathology *per se*
perhaps may be found incurable.

If specialized after-care is available, these prisoners, who may
well leave the prison in a condition worse than at the time of their
entry, may be eligible for parole. They are much more in need of expert psychiatric after-care than many others, and without this they
may quickly relapse and return to prison. Counselling sexually
deviated parolees cannot be attempted by laymen, but only by the
psychiatrist, aided by the psychiatric social worker.

Alcoholics are always very much in danger when re-entering
society. Through modern medical therapy, combined with psychotherapy, an alcoholic may be treated while in prison, but this treatment may succeed only if he continues it while on parole. One
of the most important after-care issues therefore is to ensure the
continuation of treatment.

The alcoholic is a special personality type, whose difficulty must
be understood thoroughly before supervision is undertaken. As a
rule only psychiatrists and psychiatric social workers are prepared
to deal with this difficult task, possibly in addition to those who
themselves have suffered from alcoholism, but have been cured.
Here also specialized after-care seems to be called for.

In some countries, the problem of drug addiction requires
much attention. Just as in the case of alcoholism the chronic use
of drugs creates a special personality type (as a rule based upon
already existing pathological traits) and so specialized after-care
by psychiatric after-care agencies is also necessary.

10

A SUMMARY OF PAROLE RULES*

ONE OF THE ORIGINS OF PAROLE is the eighteenth century "ticket of leave," which played an important part in the British administration of Australia as a penal settlement for transported criminals. The "ticket of leave" was a declaration by the governor of Australia which exempted a convict from further servitude and permitted him to seek private employment within a specified district.

The English Penal Servitude Act of 1853, which gave legal status to the "ticket of leave" system, substituted imprisonment for transportation and specified the length of time that prisoners had to serve before becoming eligible for conditional release on a "license to be at large." The license was granted with the following conditions:

1. The power of revoking or altering the license of a convict will most certainly be exercised in the case of misconduct.

2. If, therefore, he wishes to retain the privilege which by his good behavior under penal discipline he has obtained, he must prove by his subsequent conduct that he is really worthy of Her Majestys clemency.

3. To produce a forfeiture of the license, it is by *no* means necessary that the holder should be convicted of any new offense. If he associates with notoriously bad characters, leads an idle or dissolute life, or has no visible means of obtaining a honest livelihood, etc., it will be assumed that he is about to relapse into crime, and he will be at once apprehended and recommitted to prison under his original sentence.

ONE HUNDERD YEARS AGO

Prisoners released under the act were not supervised, it did not take long before everyone realized that the only effects of the act were confusion and disorder. A system of regular supervision and uniform procedure was urged, with prescribed rules and regulations. This was developed in the 1850's in Ireland, where the "license to be at large" was granted to a convict "from the day of his

---

*Nat R. Arluke: *National Probation and Parole Association Journal*, 2:6-13, January, 1956.

liberation under this order" for the remaining time of his sentence, except that it could be "immediately forfeited by law" if he were to be "convicted of some indictable offense within the United Kingdom" before the expiration of his sentence, or if it should "please Her Majesty sooner to revoke or alter" the license: It was noted also that "This license is given subject to the conditions endorsed upon the same, upon the breach of any of which it will be liable to be revoked, whether such breach is followed by conviction or not."

The conditions referred to were the following:

1. The holder shall preserve this license and produce it when called upon to do so by a magistrate or police officer.

2. He shall abstain from any violation of the law.

3. He shall not habitually associate with notoriously bad characters, such as reported thieves and prostitutes.

4. He shall not lead an idle and dissolute life, without means of obtaining an honest livelihood.

5. If the license is forfeited or revoked in consequence of a conviction of any felony, he will be liable to undergo a term of penal servitude equal to that portion of his term which remained unexpired when his license was granted.

6. Each convict coming to reside in Dublin City or in the County of Dublin will, within three days after his arrival, report himself at the Police Office, ... where he will receive instructions as to his further reporting himself.

7. Each convict residing in the provinces will report himself to the constabulary station of his locality within three days after his arrival and subsequently on the first of each month.

8. A convict must not change his locality without notifying the change to the locality to which he is about to proceed.

9. Any infringement of these rules by the convict will cause to be assumed that he is leading an idle, irregular life and thereby entail a revocation of his license.

Conditionally released prisoners were expected to inform their employers of their criminal record: if they failed to do so, the head of the police was responsible for transmitting the information.

That was one hundred years ago. Consider, for a moment, advances in the welfare of other groups which, like the parolee group, are made up of the scorned, the rejected, the handicapped—say, the mentally ill, or religious and racial minorities, or the economically backward. Compare changes in attitude toward these with any changes, if any, toward the parolee. Compare parole regulations of one hundred years ago with today's.

FUNDAMENTAL QUESTIONS

By and large, parole rules have continued pretty much as they were a century ago. Does this mean that they are satisfactorily meeting their purpose and therefore should not be changed? Does it suggest that there may have been changes in emphasis and interpretation, less obvious but perhaps more important than the fact that the letter of parole rules has changed very little?

Some other questions arise from an examination of parole rules: How are parole rules used? As guides? As coercive devices? As casework treatment tools? Do parole rules help in the community adjustment of the parolee or do they plague him as continuous reminders of his "second-class citizen" status? Are they pitched so high that parole adjustment is unattainable in many cases? Can we establish parole rules which give evidence of awareness of the communities' pressures on the released offender—rules and conditions tailored, as close as possible, to the needs of the parolee and his community?

If it is conceded that parole rules and conditions do not have to be immutable, how can they be modified or amended in specific cases? Should individual modifications be made by the parole officer, or by the supervisor, or by the central officer, or by the parole board?

You may have read, in *Confidential* magazine for January, 1955, an article entitled "Parole—Freedom on a String." The subheading was, "What good is a system that censors your job, bars you from women, and puts you back under arrest without cause? Parole can be an engine of torture that succeeds in redoubling hatred of law, cops, and penal 'experts.'" A large part of the public still accepts that kind of statement as gospel truth, and we continually see its imprint when we interview prospective parolees, especially those who have had no prior experience with parole. Doesn't this suggest the need for an analysis of our public relations programs so that we may erase or at least begin to minimize these erroneous impressions?

FREQUENCY OF PAROLE RULES

The chart on pages 122 and 123 summarizes the policy of each of the 48 states in regard to parolee behavior. The 24 regulations listed include all that refer explicitly to restrictions on behavior. (However, two of them—17 and 19—really indicate parole board action in the event that parolee violates his parole.)

The number of regulations indicated for a state on the chart does not necessarily coincide with the actual number in the state's official document handed to the parolee upon release from prison. In some states the references to both liquor and narcotics usage, for example, are combined as a single regulation; and in many states the document may include statements that interpret parole board administrative policy as distinct from those that describe what is and what is not allowed in parolee behavior.

It must be borne in mind, too, that a blank in the chart means only that the regulation is not printed in the state's set of rules it does not mean that the conduct referred to is ignored in practice. This gap is comprehensively covered in many states by the parolee's signifying his agreement to "abide by such special conditions of parole as may be imposed" on him by his parole officer.

In a few states the number of stipulations about parolee behavior and parole board administrative policy exceeds twenty. How many of these the parolee can reasonably be expected to remember is a question. Because of this, one of these states includes a regulation requiring the parolee to read the regulations periodically during the entire parole period!

Not a single one of the twenty-four parole regulations appears in every one of the forty-eight state documents.

The regulations are listed below, as in the chart, in the order of frequency.

1. *Use of Liquor*: Completely prohibited in 41 states; permitted, but not to excess, in 4 states. — Florida, Idaho, Michigan, and New Jersey. No restrictions in Missouri, Virginia, and West Virginia.

2. *Association or Correspondence with Persons of Poor Reputa-*

tion: "Persons of poor reputation" are specified generally as other parolees, ex-convicts, inmates of any penal institution, persons having a criminal or police record, etc. New Hampshire policy draws a fine line between association with such persons and correspondence with them, prohibiting the former but allowing the latter when permission has first been granted by the parole officer. In 38 states, both forms of conduct are prohibited; in 3 other states —Colorado, Michigan, and Minnesota—both are allowed after permission is granted. In 6 states—Iowa, Montana, New Mexico, Virginia, West Virginia, and Wyoming—the regulations ignore the matter entirely.

3. *Change of Employment or Residence:* In 39 states, permission to make such a change must first be obtained through the parole officer. It need not be obtained in 9 states—Alabama, Arizona, California, Montana, New Mexico, Oklahoma, Vermont, West Virginia, and Wyoming.

4. *Monthly Reports*: In 38 states the parolee must fill out a monthly report blank and send it to a central agency. He is not required to do so in 10 states—Alabama, Colorado, Delaware, Maryland, New Jersey, New York, North Carolina, Rhode Island, Utah, and West Virginia.

5. *Out-of-state Travel*: Allowed, after permission is granted, in 34 states; prohibited by Iowa and Montana. No restrictions in 12 states.

6. *Permission to Marry*: In 33 states a parolee desiring to marry must first obtain the consent of the parole officer. No such requirement is specified in 15 states.

7. *First Arrival Report*: In 33 states the parolee is required to report to his parole officer immediately upon arriving at his destination after release from prison; in 15 states he is not required to do so.

8. *Operation and Ownership of Motor Vehicles*: Denied, in 30 states, unless approval of parole representative is obtained; no restriction in 18 states.

9. *Use of Narcotics*: Prohibited in 28 states; permitted in 1 state—Tennessee—when approved by a physician. No restriction mentioned in 19 states.

10. *Support Dependents*: In 27 states the parolee must promise

to support his family. No regulation of this sort is specified in the printed rules in 21 states.

11. *Possession, Sale, or Use of Weapons; Obtaining a Hunting License*: Prohibited in 12 states; allowed, after permission is granted by parole officer, in 15 states. No restriction in 21 states.

12. *Travel Out of County or Community*: Allowed in 25 states upon permission of parole officer; no restriction mentioned in 23 states.

13. *Agreement to Waive Extradition*: This is a condition of parole in 19 states. No mention of it is made in 29 states .

14. *Indebtedness*: In 11 states the parolee is allowed to incur a debt only if he has permission of the parole officer. There is no such restriction in 37 states.

15. *Curfew*: In 6 states the parolee is required to be at home for the night at a "reasonable hour." Curfew for parolees is specified as 10:30 in Illinois and 11:00 in Maine. There is no curfew regulation of any sort in 40 states.

16. *Civil Rights*:Civil rights, including suffrage and the right to hold office, are lost to the parolee in 6 states; in 1 state—Alabama —they may be restored upon application and approval of the request. In 41 states no explicit mention is made of the civil rights status of the parolee.

17. *"Street Time" Credit for Parole Violator*: In 6 states the parolee who is returned to prison for violation of parole receives credit for all or part of the time he has been on parole. Such credit is not allowed or is not mentioned in the provisions of 42 states.

18. *Gambling*: Prohibited to the parolee in 5 states; no restriction mentioned in 43 states.

19. *Conviction for Felony while on Parole*: In 4 states the parolee is warned that if he is returned to prison because of a felony he commits while on parole, he will be deprived of all "street time" credit. No mention of this is made in the regulations of 44 states.

20. *Airplane License*: In 3 states—California, Maine, and Pennsylvania—the parolee must obtain his parole officer's permission to apply for a license that would allow him to operate an airplane. Not mentioned in 45 states.

21. *Report if Arrested*: In 3 states—Colorado, Maine, and New

Jersey—the parolee is required, if he is arrested, to report the arrest to his parole officer. Not mentioned in 45 states.

22. *Treatment for Venereal Disease*: In 2 states—Florida and Pennsylvannia—a parolee who has a venereal disease is compelled to take treatment for it as a condition of remaining on parole. Not mentioned in 46 states.

23. *Church Attendance*: In 2 states—Kansas and Nebraska—the parolee must attend church regularly as a condition of remaining on parole. Not mentioned in 46 states.

24. *Enlistment in Armed Forces*: In 1 state—Ohio—the parolee is required by regulation to obtain permission of the parole officer before applying for enlistment in the armed forces. Not mentioned in regulations of 47 states.

SOME CONCLUSIONS

A. Excessive Number of Regulations in Some States

As suggested above, many of the documents listing "General Conditions of Parole" contain so large a number of regulations that the value of the parolee's signature on the parole agreement is questionable.

They are further weakened when they include, as many do, quasilegal interpretations of parole board policy. The distinction between *law* and parole board *rule* should be clearly drawn in parole rule documents.

It hardly seems necessary to impose a regulation on conduct already governed by the criminal code. For example, if a state already has a law imposing penalties for the illegal sale or use of narcotics (and most states do have such a law), why make it, superfluously, a parole regulation?

B. General Impracticality of Regulations

Many of the regulations are not realistic and do not lend themselves to practical enforcement. The complete prohibition of the use of liquor by parolees in 41 states forces us into an unrealistic position that breeds violations and contempt for the value of parole supervision. It seems to me that a "Ten Commandments" form

COMPARISON OF PAROLE

	Alabama	Arizona	Arkansas	California	Colorado	Connecticut	Delaware	Florida	Georgia	Idaho	Illinois	Indiana	Iowa	Kansas	Kentucky	Louisiana	Maine	Maryland	Massachusetts
1. Liquor usage	2	2	2	2	2	2	2	4	2	4	2	2	2	2	2	2	2	2	2
2. Association or correspondence with "undesirables"	2	2	2	2	1	2	2	2	2	2	2	2		2	2	2	2	2	2
3. Change of employment or residence		1		1	1	1	1	1	1		1	1	1	1	1	1	1	1	1
4. Filing report blanks		3	3	3		3		3	3	3	3	3	3	3	3	3	3		3
5. Out-of-state travel	1		1		1		1	1		1		1	2		1	1	1	1	1
6. Contracting a new marriage	1		1	1	1		1		1	1	1	1	1	1		1	1	1	1
7. First arrival report	3		3	3	3	3		3	3	3	3	3	3		3	3	3	3	
8. Operation and ownership of motor vehicles		1	1	1	1		1		1	1	1	1		1		1	1	1	1
9. Narcotic usage	2		2	2	2		2	2	2	2	2			2	2	2	2		2
10. Support dependents	3		3				3	3	3						3	3	3	3	3
11. Possession, sale, or use of weapons; obtaining hunting license		2	2	1	2		1	2	2		2		2	2	1	1	1	1	1
12. Travel out of county or community		1	1	1			1	1	1		1	1	1						
13. Agree to waive extradition	3			3				3	3	3						3	3		
14. Indebtedness				1							1								
15. Curfew				6							10:30						11:00		
16. Civil rights	1		2	2							2						2		
17. "Street time" credit if returned as P. V.																	5	5	
18. Gambling		2						2						2					
19. No "street time" credit if convicted of felony				5															
20. Airplane license			1														1		
21. Report if arrested				3													3		
22. Treatment for venereal disease								3											
23. Church attendance																3			
24. Enlistment in armed forces																			

KEY—1. Allowed, but permission must first be obtained. 2. Prohibited. 3. Compulsory.

REGULATIONS BY STATES

Michigan	Minnesota	Mississippi	Missouri	Montana	Nebraska	Nevada	New Hampshire	New Jersey	New Mexico	New York	North Carolina	North Dakota	Ohio	Oklahoma	Oregon	Pennsylvania	Rhode Island	South Carolina	South Dakota	Tennessee	Texas	Utah	Vermont	Virginia	Washington	West Virginia	Wisconsin	Wyoming
4	2	2		2	2	2		2	4	2	2	2	2	2	2	2	2	2	2	2	2	2	2		2		2	2
1	1	2	2		2	2	2/1	2		2	2	2	2	2	2	2	2	2	2	2	2	2		2		2		
1	1	1	1		1	1		1	1		1	1	1	1		1	1	1	1	1	1	1	1		1	1		1
3	3	3	3	3	3	3	3		3			3	3	3	3	3		3	3	3	3			3	3	3	3	3
1	1	1	1	2	1		1	1		1	1		1	1	1	1	1	1		1			1		1	1		1
1	1		1		1	1	1	1		1		1	1	1	1	1	1	1		1			1		1		1	1
3	3	3	3		3			3	3	3		3	3	3	3	3			3	3			3					
1	1		1		1	1	1	1		1		1	1		1	1	1	1			1			1		1	1	
2		2			2	2		2		2	2	2	2	2	2		1	2	2			2			2			
3		3	3		3		3		3	3	3	3	3		3			3	3	3	3		3					
	1			1	1		1		2	2	1	1				2	1	2			1							
1	1		1		1	1			1	1	1	1	1		1	1	1			1			1		1	1		
	3		3		3		3		3		3	3	3							3	3							
1	1			1	1	1	1		1		1			1													1	
6						6	6			6		6																
								2				2																
							5						5									5		5				
					2														2									
							5	5		5																		
															1													
							3																					
															3													
					3																							
													1															

4. Allowed but not to excess.   5. May be received.   6. "Reasonable hour."

of agreement would provide the frame-work for more intelligent and functional supervision of parolees.

C. Lack of Uniformity

The lack of unformity is, of course, the most obvious defect of parole regulations. Consider, for example, the regulation which requires the prospective parolee to agree to waive his right to an extradition hearing in the event of his arrest in another state. There is real question about the legality of this regulation. Furthermore, if the regulation were used either universally or not at all, there would not be the confusion and expense that are now the result of the use of Form A-3, "Agreement of Prisoner When Permitted to Go to Another State," issued by the Interstate Commission on Crime in the 29 states where the extradition waiver is not included in the list of parole rules.

Some uniformity of regulations should exist among *all* states, if for no other reason than that the number of parolees living in states other than the one in which they were sentenced is increasing all the time.

Parole regulations in the 48 states should be carefully re-examined—not separately in each state, but in a coodinated fashion. Lack of uniformity, impracticality, and multiplicity of regulations are not the only defects. Others are redundancy, complexity, legal jargon, inconsistency, and irrelevancy. All of them should be eliminated in the interest of better parole.

11

PAROLE PREDICTION*
An Introductory Statement

PAROLE PREDICTION, an estimate of the probability of violation or nonviolation of parole by an offender on the basis of experience tables, was put into practical operation in 1933 in Illinois. Since the early days of prediction, many refinements of the technique have been suggested and many issues raised and discussed—for instance, the weighting of predictive factors, the comparative importance of dynamic versus static factors, evaluation of the changing attitudes of the inmates in the course of correctional process, inconsistency of predictions based on different populations of parolees, the need for continually adjusting the experience tables, attempts to develop an index of predictive efficiency, and the continued search for the most meaningful predictive factors. The perennial central problem is the comparative merit of experience tables versus the case study in deciding on the parole of an individual offender. The conclusion that parole cannot forgo the advantages to be gained from the development and judicious use of experience tables seems to be warranted.

The term "parole prediction" is firmly established in American correctional parlance. It refers to the estimate of probability of violation or nonviolation of parole by an offender on the basis of experience tables, developed with regard to groups of offenders possessing similar characteristics.

If used without reference to this historically established specific connotation, the term might mean a number of different things. It could mean any kind of prediction of parole outcome. For instance, parole prediction could mean some kind of intuitive prognosis with regard to a particular offender. It could also mean a common-sense prognosis. On the other hand, it could be derived from an assessment of the personality as a whole, based on the expertness of a behavioral scientist or group of scientists evaluating the

*Peter P. Lejins: *Crime and Delinquency*. National Council on Crime and Delinquency, *8*:209-214, July, 1962.

chances of success on parole by means of structured qualitative analysis which rests on some theory of human behavior and perhaps draws on similar material as illustrations. Such an assessment is often suggested as a desirable or even indispensable addition to parole prediction in the conventional sense; i.e., the computation of the chances of success on the basis of past experience with parolees.

The use of the experience tables for estimating the chances of success of a parolee or a particular type of parolee is, of course, a special application of a general method that has been used by social science, especially applied social science, for quite some time. That this method would sooner or later find its way also into the studies of criminal behavior was to be expected. Although it is in wide use, the standard reference usually is to the computation of insurance rates on the basis of experience tables.

Although the computation of experience tables and their use for prediction purposes in parole has so far been by far the most popular kind of prediction in criminology, it is, of course, only a special instance of prediction of criminal or delinquent behavior in general. Other types of prediction in this area that have also received a considerable amount of attention are prediction of probation outcome, delinquent behavior, recurrence of criminal behavior in general (recidivism) , etc.

EARLY HISTORY

In 1923, Professor Sam Bass Warner, of Harvard, describing a pioneering study that attempted to relate the background factors available in the reformatory records of a group of offenders to success or failure on parole, reported only a very limited relationship. A few months later Professor Hornell Hart suggested that improved methodology would reveal the relationship which Warner failed to find and that several background factors which *singly* do not show a significant relationship with the ultimate parole outcome should be *combined* into a prognostic score. By reason of these suggestions Hart is widely credited as the originator of the parole prediction idea.

Development of a table of expectancy rates of parole violation and nonviolation and introduction of this instrument into actual use in a state parole system was accomplishment of Professor Ernest W. Burgess, of Chicago University, and his associates. Reported in 1928 and subsequently put to use in Illinois, it was the first large-scale study of the relationship of the offender's background factors to the parole outcome, and for many years it served as the basis for the accumulation of data and for further studies by a number of scholars.

Briefly, Professor Burgess' parole prediction procedure was as follows:

Within a parolee population for which the average violation rate was known, the violation rates for sub-populations possessing some specific background characteristic were computed; e.g., the rate for parolees characterized by "no previous work record," for parolees with a record of "casual work," for those with a record of "irregular work," and for those with a record of "regular work." Where these violation rates were lower than the violation rate for the entire parolee population, the corresponding factor was considered to be a favorable or positive one. All positive factors were placed into an experience table and each candidate for parole was given one point for each such factor in his background. Finally, a table giving the violation expectancy rate for offenders with different numbers of favorable factors was worked out for the population studied. It was assumed that future candidates for parole would have the same chance of success as those having the same number of favorable factors in the original population.

In this prototypic expectancy table the chances of success ran from 98.5 per cent, for parolees having sixteen to twenty-one favorable factors, to 24 per cent for those having only two, three, or four favorable factors. This instrument was put into practice in Illinois in 1933.

Publication of Burgess' proposals was followed soon afterward by Sheldon and Eleanor Glueck's report of what is usually regarded as another pioneer advance in the development of instruments predicting criminal behavior. The Gluecks took a somewhat different course and continued independently of the Burgess-Illinois tradition. The essentially new thought for prediction already evident in their first publications was the weighting of the favorable background factors on the basis of the extent of their relationship to success or failure. These weights can be and have been developed through various statistical techniques.

Even in these early stages of investigation the idea was expressed that the experience tables should be used not only for the computation of the chances of success of parole, but also as guides in deciding on the kind of supervision or treatment to be given the released parolee.

LATER MAJOR IDEAS

An important addition to the rationale of parole prediction is Laune's observation, in *Predicting Criminality,* that almost all the background factors in the Burgess-type experience table are static; that is, not subject to change by the institutional treatment program. For example, pre-incarceration work history, marital status, national or ethnic origin, etc., remain the same, regardless of what is done to the offender in the way of treatment. This means that the correctional process—preparation of the offender for his return to the community—had hardly any role at all in prediction. Laune suggested that the changes produced in the inmate in the course of institutional treatment be accounted for in the expectancy table, thus introducing into the treatment process a certain element of dynamism—and also, some would say, optimism. He tried to discover the attitudes of the inmate through the "hunches" of fellow inmates, who presumably know, better than the institution's personnel, what these attitudes are. While Laune's reasearch is important, the follow-up of his study showed that the inmate-hunch method was no more effective than the original Burgess method.

Of the score of other criminoligists in the thirties who were interested in parole prediction, one might limit mention to Clark Tibbitts, George B. Vold, and Barkev S. Sanders. Their principal contribution was the discovery that parolee experiences—or predictions derived from different populations of parolees—were not always consistent; it was possible, they said, that rapid changes in administrative practices and policies and in the general conditions of life could change the role of the background factors quite rapidly.

Later this problem was picked up by Lloyd E. Ohlin, who also discovered, in a comprehensive study of Illinois parole, the need for continuously adjusting the experience tables. Ohlin maintained that research on predictive factors ought to be a part of the parole system and that it be a constant operation, to the extent that experience of parolees who have completed the first year of parole should be used in evaluating parolee backgrounds the next year. This means the development of a very sensitive instrument, quite different from what the original researchers probably had in mind.

As Karl F. Schuessler suggested in his attempt to structure the history of parole prediction by distinguishing several stages in its development, the post-World War II period was characterized by exploration of methodological refinement. Of these the most significant were conducted by Ohlin and his associates. Especially noteworthy is the Ohlin and Duncan "index of predictive efficiency." This measure consists of a percentage change in the prediction error as the result of using an experience table instead of the overall rate.

Another refinement, also brought in by Ohlin after study of the Illinois materials, was reduction of the number of favorable factors originally developed by Burgess. A more sophisticated statistical analysis of the relative weight of these factors as predictors of the behavior of the parolee demonstrated that, for practical purposes, twelve factors would be as effective as the original twenty-one. These explorations further showed the relative importance of just one or two factors among these twelve.

USE BY PAROLE BOARDS

It is now time to turn to the all-important question of the applicability of the experience tables to the action of the paroling authority in an individual case.

This has been a crucial and controversial issue from the very beginning of parole prediction. The issue, characteristic of the social sciences in general, is simply this: prediction based on the experience tables are never 100 per cent correct and often fall far below. This means there is always the possibility that a certain individual, denied parole on the basis of the unfavorable past experiences of others with similar backgrounds, may be just the one who, in spite of this similarity, would not act as the majority did in the past. Refusing him parole would then constitute an injustice, of course, and at the same time an operational error.

The opposition to the use of prediction tables, on the basis of the probability sketched above, is made up of two camps. One consists of those who, hardly understanding what it is all about, clamor that the fate of an individual should not be decided on the basis of "statistics"; the other consists of those who thoroughly understand the meaning of the manipulations involved and are justifiably concerned about the proper application of experience tables to individual cases.

From the beginning many have maintained that recommendations based on experience tables should be supplemented by a thorough case study. Several researches were conducted in an attempt to shed some light on this issue. Some of these showed a remarkable similarity between predictions read from the experience tables and those derived from a diagnosis made, for example, by a psychiatrist; others failed to establish such reassuring coincidence in the results produced by the two methods. A good discussion of the relationship between the case study and the prognosis based on experience tables can be found in Leslie Wilkins' *What Is Prediction and Is It Necessary in Evaluating Treatment?*

There are no signs of an end to the battle between the intransigents—on one hand, those who are obsessed in their opposition to statistical prediction "as a matter of principle," and, on the other, those who think that any parole selection procedure other than statistical prediction belongs in the same class as the talisman, the divining rod, and the wishbone. It is probably safe to state that, apart from these extremists, the vast majority of professionals in parole would agree that the opportunities offered by the experience tables could not and should not be missed.

Just as in other fields where computation of categoric risks has been found useful—as, for instance, in insurance and the assaying of aptitudes—so also in parole we cannot afford to forgo the help offered by the summation of experiences with types of offenders similar to the one whose case is under discussion. With the exception, perhaps, of the extreme ends of the continuum, a case study will always be necessary. The experience tables, however, would add considerably to the perspective on the idiosyncracies of the individual case and can serve as a guide for the exploration of the danger zones both during the formulation of the parole decision and during the subsequent treatment.

Parole prediction devices should be further explored and refined. I am convinced that they are destined to become an important part of the groundwork for parole decisions.

12

SOME DANGERS IN PAROLE PREDICTION*

As prediction techniques are perfected and increasingly used, uncertain incongruities existing between parole theory and parole prediction may have detrimental effects on parole itself. The inadequacies of substandard parole jurisdictions may become less evident if only good risks are released; challenge to professional skills may be reduced; the administrative advantages inherent in prediction may supersede correctional ends; the principle of individualized treatment may be threatened. The best use to which prediction can be put is in the identification of prisoners whose parole tends to bring this measure into public disrepute.

T HE INTELLECTUAL challenge and excitement of parole prediction research has drawn to it some of the best minds in American and European academic criminology. In a discipline long frustrated in its causation research by the knotty problems of definition, sampling, concept construction, and research design, prediction work stands as a fertile and tempting islet upon whose soil the statistically oriented social scientists are bringing to fruition projects close to the dual aims of all scientific endeavor: prediction and control. The continued development and refinement of parole prediction devices and an increase in their practical application seem extremely likely to me. The various problems yet to be solved—unreliability of prison records, the need to precisely measure attitude and character traits, the present inability to correct for disparity between the social milieux of the experience table parolees and the future milieux of the predicted parolees, to name a few—are largely technical. Their solution within the next ten years or so seems possible in view of the rapid advances being made in statistics, computer technology, social research methods, and the behavioral sciences.

*Ralph W. England, Jr.: *National Council on Crime and Delinquency Journal, 8:* 265-269, July, 1962.

My reservations about the use of parole prediction devices are not based, therefore, upon their present transitional shortcomings, but upon what I regard as the very nature of their application, which is inimical to sound correctional theory and practice.

INADEQUATE PAROLE PERPETUATED

Parole theory emphasizes that adequate parole entails positive, constructive efforts by trained and experienced persons who work, within a favorable procedural and community setting, in the behalf of ex-prisoners. In practice, of course, few state parole systems can boast of meeting "ideal" standards: caseloads are too heavy; many officers do not meet professional qualifications; community facilities lack adequate referral services; politics intrude. Progress in meeting good standards of parole can be seriously impeded if the practice becomes widespread of paroling only those prisoners who can "survive" what are, in general, substandard parole conditions. The shortcomings of a poorly trained physician can be ignored if he has only healthy patients. The use of high-quality prediction devices within low-quality parole jurisdictions will make possible the accurate selection of low-risk cases for parole, thus virtually guaranteeing that these areas will eventually boast high success rates. This may already be afoot in Illinois, a state which has pioneered in the routine use of prediction devices but which is not known for its outstanding parole system. Reported parole violation rates declined from 57 per cent in 1926 to 26 per cent in 1943, with a shift from a preponderance of major to a preponderance of minor violations. At the same time, however, the proportion of Illinois prisoners released on parole declined from 69.3 per cent in 1926 to as low as 38 per cent in 1952; by 1960 it had climbed to 51.9 per cent but was still considerably lower than the proportion of prisoners paroled in four neighboring states.

Common sense would lead one to believe that the quality of parole that a released man experiences would have some causal connection with success or failure, and that prediction devices should take cognizance of this connection by including factor categories pertaining to parole quality. However, the methodology of prediction prohibits such inclusion because prisoners who have had no previous parole experience cannot be scored in these categories. Consequently, prediction devices must operate not only as though parole quality were *uniform* for every parolee released within a particular jurisdiction but also as though the quality were sufficient to assure success, providing the prisoner's prior characteristics do not predispose him otherwise. Given the present structuring of prediction devices, failure on parole cannot be attributed to inadequacies in the parole process. Thus, parole as a corrective measure is insulated from being spotlighted as a variable in success or failure.

PREDICTION AND PROFESSIONAL CHALLENGE

Fundamental to the morale of the trained and qualified parole agent is the challenge of working with parolees who, without his assistance, stand a good chance of becoming recidivists. Professionals worthy of the label—whether in law, medicine, theology, accounting, engineering, or correction—thrive on problems requiring practical application of the theoretical underpinnings of their callings. Purely routine matters can be relegated to technicians; professionals deal with complex and problematical situations whose solutions require the exercise of talents far transcending those needed for technical operations. To "take the risk out of parole" by releasing only those estimated to be good bets would reduce parole to a merely technical level for which the limited talents of office clerks and policemen-turned-parole-agents would suffice.

My hunch is that most low-risk prisoners, as determined by prediction devices, are those who, so far as their recidivist tendencies are concerned, should not have been imprisoned at all. That they *are* imprisoned testifies to the continuing archaic demand by legal authorities and the public for punishment and example-setting rather than to the judges' perception that these convicted persons need rehabilitation in prison. If this hunch is correct, parole agents whose clients are picked for them by prediction tables are serving as unwitting handmaidens to punitive rather than correctional ends. Nothing in parole theory countenances this decidedly nonprofessional function. Quite the opposite. High-risk prisoners with decided criminal leanings are those most desperately in need of whatever truly rehabilitative resources a state can provide, *including professional parole.* Ironically, prediction devices encourage parole releases at the wrong end of the risk spectrum.

AN ADMINISTRATIVE AID ONLY

The indigenous conservatism of administrative bodies, with their desire for smooth, uneventful operations and their avoidance of the problematical and risky, will I fear, lead an increasingly perfected parole prediction technique to function wholly as an administrative rather than as a correctional instrument—to the ultimate detriment of parole. One solid virtue of the present "clinical guess" system now in use (whose predictive power is, for the time being, not very different from today's relatively crude prediction tables) is that it embodies an *uncertain* degree of risk—an uncertainty which may be promoting greater use of parole today than we can ultimately expect.

Not all parole boards are charged with direct responsibility for field operations; their members are not, strictly speaking, administrators, but they share with the administration the fact that their release decisions are open to public scrutiny and judgment. While routine decisions made by other state officials are obscured by the complexities of government operations, those of parole boards can at any time be brought sensationally to public attention, especially their "wrong" decisions in releasing men who later commit heinous crimes. Although the furor created by such cases sometimes results in unfair criticism of parole boards, the criticism is keenly felt in several echelons of government and can have serious political reprecussions.

Both in prison and on parole an offender is presumably undergoing treatment. Parole theory does not define parole as a "testing" of the offender's capacity for conventional behavior but rather as a continuation of corrective measures begun during incarceration. But parole prediction does not in any sense predict *progress* through a correctional program; rather, it gives the odds that an untoward incident (usually a technical violation or a new offense) will or will not occur. Moreover, parole prediction operates on the assumption that parole *is* a testing period, and it implements this erroneous assumption by selecting for release those prisoners least likely to fail

the test. Why isn't equal encouragement given to predicting untoward incidents during imprisonment—which, after all, is simply a
preceding stage in the correctional process? The answer is, I think,
that disapproved behavior in prison has few public repercussions;
even if this were so, the public would be hard put to identify the
responsible prison officials and accuse them of bad judgment. Parole
prediction's greatest value is its power to maximize administrative
tranquility and to minimize embarrassment to paroling officials.
Placing such a tool in their hands would, it seems to me, initiate a
chain of events leading in an entirely opposite direction from the
one specified by parole theory.

PREDICTION VS. INDIVIDUALIZATION

The American Correctional Association has defined parole as
"a procedure by which prisoners are selected for release *on the basis
of individual response and progress within the correctional institution* and a service by which they are provided with necessary
controls and guidance as they serve the remainder of their sentences
within the free community." Clearly reflected here are the ideas
that imprisonment and parole are continuous parts of a corrective
process and that a prisoner cannot reasonably pass from one to the
next until sufficient progress within the first stage has been made.
While the supporters of prediction could claim that measurements
of institutional progress are *indirectly* incorporated into prediction
devices (since the "good" and "bad" parole risks are prisoners whose
progress has been, respectively, sufficient and insufficient), this exceedingly awkward and remote measure is wholly adventitious.
Moreover, the development of good prediction tables does not
necessarily entail the development of measures of progress through
an institutional program because such measures are not directly relevant to the prediction researcher's hunt for reliable, valid, and efficient predictors. Most predictive factors in studies made during
the last twenty years have been drawn from the pre-incarceration
period of the subjects' lives: work history, previous convictions,
character type. The few factors that have been derived from prison
experiences were selected solely because they proved to be good
predictors.

Parole decisions made by exclusive use of prediction devices (an inherent tendency as their perfection nears) would *not* require assessments of "individual response and progress within the correctional institution." This difficult and exacting task is neatly side-stepped and an important canon of individual treatment violated.

Ideally, *every* prisoner released from a correctional institution should go out under supervision; the practice of holding some offenders to the expiration of their terms until "their debt is paid" is an exercise in futility. Practically, however, this policy would be difficult to implement in most jurisdictions, public sentiment being what it is. Sooner or later some paroles prove so extraordinarily unpopular that impractical idealism might only jeopardize the needed liberalization of parole. But what are these unpopular paroles? What offenses are involved? What kinds of individuals? Under what circumstances does their unpopularity become manifest? The greatest service prediction researchers could perform for parole would be to construct tables identifying those prisoners whose parole tends to bring this measure into disrepute.

CONCLUSIONS

The general business of handling behavioral deviants–including those we label criminal—is still largely unscientific. Correction especially is an unsettled amalgam of ideas and practices accumulated over the last several centuries. Stone walls and iron bars enclose fluorescent lights and psychologists' pastel quarters; prisoners sentenced under the stern aegis of public moral condemnation are subjected to sympathetic personal-social evaluation; a magistrate's momentary dyspepsia sends one vagrant to a house of correction and another back to the street; old and new theories of rehabilitation compete for administrative support. Whether or not these diverse and often incompatible elements will eventually be replaced by a coherent configuration based on scientific principles, the fact remains that thrusting into the *present* amalgam a device far more rational (in the sense of being empirically based) than the enterprise it would purportedly assist may invite some entirely unanticipated kinds of trouble. An interesting aspect of parole prediction is that it can be developed quite independently of correctional standards, since neither its logic nor its methods arise from correctional theory any more than do those, say, of mathematics. The intellectual fascination of prediction, with its elegant models, its amenability to quantification, and its limitless practical possibilities, does not in itself qualify it as a friend of good correction. Its potentials for blocking the further improvement of parole, reducing parole to a technical level, increasing the timorousness of parole boards, and obscuring the need for individual treatment may, in fact, result in its becoming good parole's worst enemy.

13

CURRENT THINKING ON PAROLE PREDICTION TABLES*

I N THE PAST quarter-century, tests have been developed to measure intelligence, special abilities, emotional states, and social attitudes; to discover the personal and situational elements associated with successful performance of an activity, i.e., which factors are significantly relevant to success or failure; to predict success in school, work, marriage, and military service; and to identify predelinquent children.

The predictive method has also been developed for parole selection. Its actuarial instruments—referred to as prediction scales, prediction statistics, expectancy tables, and experience tables—are not a recent innovation. As long ago as 1928 Professor Ernest W. Burgess, of the University of Chicago, wrote: "The practical value of an expectancy table should be as useful in parole administration as similar rates have proved to be in insurance."

Noting the growth in knowledge of factors related to parole success and failure, Burgess held that is was possible to predict parole behavior. The paroling authority would do its job more effectively, he maintained, if it had available a reliable indication of the probabilities of violation on parole for different classes of offenders.

Sociologist-actuaries believe today that the probable outcome of parole can be predicted by experience tables. Those working closely with such tables assert that research has steadily improved their accuracy in predicting parole outcome.

Prediction tables are developed by systematic study of factors closely identified with parole success and failure. Each inmate is scored on the basis of this series of factors, and predictions are made on the basis of the score. To learn how prediction tables are developed, tested, and applied in parole selection, read Ohlin's *Selection for Parole*. It should be in the library of every parole board member, penal administrator, and correctional worker.

---

*Victor H. Evjen: *National Council on Crime and Deliquency Journal, 8*:215-238, July, 1962.

The goal in parole prediction, according to Ohlin, is "to in-crease the number of paroles granted to offenders who are likely to succeed on parole and correspondingly to reduce the number granted to those who are likely to fail." "As this is accomplished," he continues, "violations will not adversely affect the parole pos-sibilities of future applicants." Parole prediction methods deter-mine the chances a person has of making a successful or unsuccess-ful adjustment after release from a penal institution. They are not designed to give the optimum time for release or to portend respon-siveness to supervision.

BOARDS' USE OF PREDICTION TABLES

To learn the extent to which paroling authorities use predic-tion statistics in parole selection, I sent a form letter, in August, 1961, to the parole boards of the fifty states and several other juris-dictions. The letter asked these two questions:

1. Have prediction statistics (schedules, ratings, etc.) ever been used by your Board in the selection parolees?
2. Does your paroling authority use prediction devices at the present time? If so, please indicate briefly the manner in which they are used.

Of the forty-eight states responding, forty-four indicated they had never used prediction statistics in parole selection and are not now using them.

The U.S. Board of Parole, the New York City Parole Com-mission, and the paroling authorities of Puerto Rico, Canada, the U.S. Army, and the District of Columbia also answered "No" to each question.

Illinois has had nearly thirty years of experience with predic-tion tables. And it is the only state in which a routine system of parole prediction has been established. Since 1933 a sociologist-actuary at each of the major penal institutions has been conducting research in parole prediction and selection and has prepared for the parole board a routine prediction report on each inmate appearing for a parole hearing. He computes the prisoner's statistical chances of making a successful adjustment on parole. The final sentence in the report reads: "This inmate is in a class in which ——— per cent may be expected to violate the parole agreement." Together with sociological, psychiatric, and psychological reports, and interviews by the Board, the probability score is used as an aid in selecting prisoners for parole. The Joliet-Stateville and Menard branches of the Illinois State Penitentiary have one prediction table; the Pontiac branch for "younger improvable offenders" has another. The women's institution at Dwight has none. The tables used at Joliet were originally developed by Burgess (1928) and modified by Ohlin (1951 and 1954). The table now used at Pontiac was developed by Daniel Glaser (1954).

In Ohio a parole prediction index has been developed under the direction of Dr. John Pruski, member of the Pardon and Parole Commission, from a constellation of variables obtained from responses on the Minnesota Multiphasic Personality Inventory (MMPI). Inmate testing under this system began in September, 1961.

In California the Youth Authority and the Department of Corrections have begun an extensive program of establishing "base expectancy" scores, which will be used in parole selection when they become standardized and perfected.

In Colorado the Parole Board, according to Edward W. Grout, Executive Director of the State Department of Parole, is now developing prediction statistics.

In Minnesota, the St. Cloud Reformatory experimented with the Ohlin Prediction Report in the fifties; prediction tables are not used in the state at present.

EXPERTS' COMMENTS ON PREDICTION

Last July I wrote to fifty leaders in criminology, penal and correctional administration, and parole, asking each to give in about 200 words his opinion about prediction devices and their place in parole selection. My purpose, the letter explained, was merely to present a poll of reactions to prediction statistics.

Replies were received from 44 persons: 24 criminologists and sociologists (to whom I have assigned the symbol "C"); 11 parole board members ("PB"); 8 prison administrators ("P"); and 1 probation administrator ("PR"). Nine of the respondents are authors of criminology texts.

Of the 44 who replied, 33 (75 per cent) believe in the potential value of prediction tables (C-16; PB-9; P-7; PR-1) ; 11 question the value of prediction statistics (C-8; PB-2; P-1) . Their thoughts on parole prediction statistics are summarized below; the complete text of the remarks of 35 respondents is in the Appendix. Though the survey was somewhat limited and the summary is necessarily brief, I hope they will help to pave the way for a renewed, continuous, systematic study of prediction statistics and their place in selection.

These are the general comments offered:

Supporting Arguments

Prediction tables may be used as a useful guide to check one's own thinking (C-15; PB-8; P-3) . They are an aid to judgment— not a substitute for judgment. As Professor Sheldon Glueck states in his reply:

> It needs to be emphasized, because it is too often overlooked by critics, that the creators of prediction devices do not urge that such tables be applied in any mechanical, routine fashion; they are adjuncts to both the individual case history and individual experience of the parole board member. . . .

Fred Finsley, chairman of the California Adult Authority, writes:

> The mechanical predictive tables can sort out and place into categories an abundance of objective data which, if used in conjunction with skilled interviewing, can bring about much better results than either the subjective interview or the prediction table alone. The combined use of both methods can bring us much nearer to a scientific approach to sound parole release procedures.

Prediction tables give consideration to factors which the board may overlook (C-2; P-1) . It is very difficult to keep in mind all relevant factors in a case. Apportioning weights to each factor cannot be done satisfactorily without statistical techniques. Some factors are unduly overemphasized and others underemphasized. Board members have a tendency to base predictions on one factor to the exclusion of others. On this point, Professor Thorsten Sellin says:

Experience has shown that the risk of recidivism depends on many factors in the life history of prisoners. Neither intuition nor "common sense" can evaluate these factors adequately; they can be disclosed by research that seeks to correlate them with the degree of adjustment on parole. It is such research that has led to the development of actuarial, experience; or "prediction" tables of which those in use in Illinois furnish an example.

Experience as a board member is not enough (C-1) . J. Douglas Grant, a research psychologist, puts it this way:

The whole correctional field must start being systematic about observing its experience. The days when programs can be defended on the expertise of eighteen years' experience alone are rapidly being eliminated. We will hear more of such statements as, "When you say you have eighteen years' experience, you mean you have had one year's experience eighteen times." Researchers and the public, if not correctional managers, are rapidly becoming aware that experience without systematic study and feedback may only mean that the same errors are repeated for many, many years.

Individualization—the careful study of each case—depends on hunches (C-1) . Board members, at times, will make decisions on hunches without realizing or admitting they are based on hunches.

Prediction tables help to show board members where they erred in judgment (C-1; PB-1) . A systematic effort to test the judgments of parole board members not only will help to determine wherein their decisions are correct, but also will lead to improvement in prediction tables.

Prediction scores may serve as a guide to the intensiveness of supervision (C-1) . Those with a high probability of success will not need as intensive supervision as those who do not have high scores.

SOME QUESTIONS AND DOUBTS

The prediction score is for groups and may not fit the specific prisoner about whom a decision must be made (C-6; PB-1; PR-1) . Actuarial predictions apply to groups—not to prisoner X. They do not tell what will happen to a specific prisoner. The violation rate is for a particular class and its application to a prisoner falling in this class may be erroneous.

Experience tables are not universally applicable (C-2). Tables cannot be applied to different kinds of populations at different points in time. As Burgess and Sellin suggest in the Introduction to Ohlin's *Selection for Parole*:

> It is highly desirable to try out in other states the items of background, personality, and prison behavior found to be significant in Illinois. Do these items have general applicability or are they limited to Illinois and perhaps to adjoining states?

Experience tables have to be revised and tested periodically to meet changing conditions and circumstances (P-1; C-2). Factors which are highly predictive at one time may not be at another. As Burgess and Sellin point out, research must be conducted to determine whether predictive items "retain their efficiency through time" and whether "economic and social changes in our society decrease or render null and void the predictive value of items earlier found to have predictive significance."

"It is becoming increasingly clear," says Ohlin, "that routine readjustment of an experience table is required if the table is to retain its usefulness. The experience table reflects the parole conditions which existed for a sample of parolees in a certain period." Changes in parole board policies and in the nature and extent of prerelease preparation and parole supervision, and such major social and economic changes as a depression or a war, of course, affect the tables and make it necessary to adjust them. It is my understanding that at one time in Illinois, new experience tables were computed annually.

"Every few years," says Glueck, "prediction tables should be renovated by a systematic checkup on their actual effectiveness because both correctional facilities and community aid to parolees undergo change with time."

The problem is to develop a system for keeping abreast of these changes.

The information from which the tables are developed is limited (C-2). Prediction tables cannot be sounder than the information on which they are based. What goes into the computation will determine the reliability of the scores. The value, significance, and reliability of data in presentence investigation reports, classification summaries at institutions, and parole reports depend to a large extent on the qualifications of the probation, prison, and parole officers who supply these data. Their reports often lack objectivity and completeness. As one sociologist has remarked: "Opinions, hearsay, and haphazardly recorded judgments still constitute the bulk of many parole files."

Some good risks are overlooked and some poor risks are granted parole (C-1). Failures occur in the groups with higher scores and some parolees succeed even though they are in the lower-score groups. Some with high predictive scores may be highly dangerous to themselves and the community.

Some persons argue, says Glueck, that prediction tables should not be used because they predict correctly in only 80 to 90 per cent of the cases and therefore subject the remainder to the hazard of false prognosis. Such an argument, he emphasizes, overlooks the greater hazard they are subjected to by the hunch method of parole selection.

Prediction scales consider only past and present factors (C-3; PB-1; P-1). They do not take into account unforeseen situations and circumstances which contribute to either success or failure. They cannot take into consideration the special stresses and strains experienced by the parolee in his attempts to make a satisfactory parole adjustment.

"An unexpected, severe, and prolonged increase in unemployment in the area to which a parolee is released," Austin H. MacCormick reminds us, "may outweigh a half-dozen favorable factors."

Several others pointed out that there is little use in predicting future conduct in terms of present attitudes.

Prediction tables do not sufficiently consider the seriousness of the offense and the likelihood that the prospective parolee will repeat the offense (C-1). Certain offenders, such as forgers and counterfeiters, have high recidivism rates.

Despite the prediction score, the parole board cannot ignore the feelings of the community (PB-2). The board, particularly where it is the target of criticism, must be sensitive to public attitudes; it must take account of the public reaction toward certain crimes; it must consider not only the readiness of the prisoner for parole, but also the willingness of the community to accept him as a parolee. The nature of the crime, for example, may preclude parole even though the perpetrator scores high on the prediction table.

In some jurisdictions the grant or denial of parole may be decided by the influence exerted on the board by prominent persons in the community.

The tables overlook subjective elements not easily measured (PR-1; PB-2; C-2; P-1). A person's behavior is a complex of intangibles—his attitudes and feelings, his sense of values, his concept of self—which do not lend themselves to computation. Prediction tables, in general, do not take into account the dynamic interplay of the many elements of an inmate's circumstances, relationships, and situations. Statistical prediction in its present stage of development, say Burgess and Sellin, deals with the external rather than the subjective aspects of behavior. Intensive study is needed, they assert, to probe into the prisoner's subjective life.

Walter M. Wallack, a warden of long experience, declares:

> From what I know about the method of deriving prediction formulae, I have no confidence in their reliability as an instrument for determining whether an individual should be paroled. There are too many intangibles involved. Some of the factors ....cannot be reduced to objectivity.

Only clinical insight can interpret and predict (C-6; PB-1). "Formulae based on statistical correlations are no substitute for clinical insight," says Howard B. Gill. Individual consideration is required. There is no substitute for the careful study of each case.

Frederick Hoefer, formerly a parole board member, writes that "prediction devices should never be used as a mechanical substitute for individual case study. This is particularly true when we make a decision granting or denying parole." Hoefer continues:

> A strong warning is in order against any attempt to substitute arithmetic for judgment when making a decision concerning a human life. Individual case study by trained professional workers is the only possible basis [for such decisions]. . . . The case analyst, after completing his study and evaluation of the case, could use a prediction table as a control device to check his own thinking and to see if he has overlooked an important element in the case.

Russell G. Oswald says:

Aside from the obvious limitations of a strictly actuarial approach in the profession of rehabilitating persons, there are always other considerations which demand that the paroling authority rely on its own evaluation of each individual. Among the other considerations are the nature of the crime, the adequacy of the parole program, the kind of parole supervision available, and, finally and most importantly, the conviction of professional parole practitioners that the parole of any person is a matter requiring individual consideration.

We are dealing with personalities, not digits (C-1). Professor Negley K. Teeters says:

Another serious limitation of mechanical parole techniques is that the parole petitioner is a person, not a mere digit, and this presents a hazard of losing sight of him as a living personality. Prediction charts nullify that indefinable, yet precious quality some parole officers may have which we call insight, a quality that must be accepted in any human interaction.

Sociologist J. P. Shalloo puts it this way:

We might suggest computers or electronic historicometers in conjunction with futurometers and we could all sit back and let the vibrations take over to warn and predict. Sounds fantastic? Well, the whole mechanical trend is just that. Prisoners were once numbers. Now they may become holes in a card, and so will their relatives!

There are too many individual differences for human conduct to be predicted with a high degree of accuracy (P-1; C-1). Significant experiences and influences in both the prison and the free community and the different ways in which different personalities respond to them make it difficult to predict how successful a person may be on parole. Supporting this position, Wallack states that "No two conduct patterns are ever developed in exactly the same way. Heredity and environmental pressures always result in a unique outcome in the development of individual human conduct."

Judgment of the paroling authority is more reliable than a mathematical probability (P-1; PB-1; C-1). Wallack asserts that the total experience and common-sense judgment of paroling officials is more reliable than any formula based on mathematical probability. "This is not to say," he states, "that sometime in the future it will not be possible to find some significant assistance in forming a judgment as to whether or not to parole by means of one of these newfangled, terrifically expensive 'thinking machines.' " He believes "it will always be necessary for one or more human beings to dominate in the judgment as to what might be expected in the conduct of any member of the human race."

Commenting on the judgment of parole board members, Ohlin makes the following observation:

> An examination of the factors in the parole decision leads to the conclusion that no single device which social scientists may contrive can adequately supplant the mature and considered judgment of the parole board members. This judgment is on sounder ground when sociological, psychological, and psychiatric knowledge of the offender is fully used. No one of these single sources of information, however, is in a position to encompass all the implications of a case for the individual and society.

Prediction tables do not account for the impact of prison life on the parolee and for differences in the effectiveness of supervision under different parole agents (C-5; P-1; PB-1). Uneven supervision prevails.The skills, insight, and knowledge of the parole agent and the adequacy of the overall parole program may determine to a large extent whether a person makes good on parole.

A career prison administrator writes: "Are we to assume that what happens to a man in the institution and the type of supervision he receives on parole has nothing to do with whether he succeeds or fails?" Any intelligent selection procedure, he emphasizes, takes these factors into account.

The tables rely on a single criterion of success—namely, recidivism (C-3). As a yardstick for measuring parole failure, the parole violation warrant is clear and objective, but, as several pointed out, it is also unreliable.

Parole violation warrants are issued for a variety of reasons—alleged commission of a crime, drifting back to associations with known criminals, rebellious behavior, mental deviations, and a host of others. The parolee might even be returned to prison for correction of a physical defect which cannot be cared for in the local community.

Some violation warrants are issued for technical infractions and others for convictions on new offenses. Some of these new offenses are misdemeanors of no serious consequence—offenses for which a large proportion of so-called "law-abiding" citizens are brought to court.

In some instances warrants are issued on the first violation without regard to the relative seriousness of the violation. Some parole officers request a parole warrant at the drop of a hat. Others consider technical infractions relatively unimportant. There are those who play ostrich to hold down violation rates!

Board members and parole officers alike have biases against certain offenses and personality types; their blind spots are reflected in their action on parole violations.

Some boards may have other criteria—such as a continued pattern of criminality or a reasonably good social adjustment—for determining parole outcome. But there is, in general, a lack of agreement as to what constitutes adjustment. As Ohlin emphasizes, prediction systems based on different measures of success would not predict the same event. The important problem in parole prediction, he points out, is to decide which measure of success would prove most practicable for regular use in a correctional system.

A parole board may have reason to believe a person may commit the same offense if paroled, but it cannot tell to what extent a parolee may be involved in technical infractions of his parole conditions. Violation warrants are frequently issued for these infractions. In most jurisdictions these infractions are counted as violations in the same manner as warrants issued charging a new offense.

On this question, Gill writes:

> Although recidivism is the most obvious measure of success in prison work, because it is subject to so many intervening variables it is also the most unreliable. Nevertheless, in order to produce a quick and easy method of insuring popular approval in parole selection, base expectancy analyses have been developed which classify offenders according to risk of recidivism. Thus the vagaries of parole supervision rather than change in criminal tendencies based on individual treatment determine parole selection.

Parole boards would tend to rely solely on the prediction tables (C-2). One criminologist expresses concern as to "whether prediction tables might not give parole agencies a false sense of proficiency and security, discouraging the use of case studies and causing officials to lose sight of the prisoner as a living and changing personality." As has already been pointed out, those who are responsible for developing actuarial tables would be the first to say that the grant or denial of parole cannot be made entirely on the basis of the probability score.

Prediction instruments are too technical (C-2). One respondent says most parole boards show a negative attitude toward prognostic tables, which, they say, are too technical. It is human nature to want to avoid what is difficult to understand. Exposure to an area of knowledge beyond our field of competence makes us uncomfortable.

One author of a criminology text believes that the reluctance of parole agencies to employ prediction tables is caused by "the confusing categories and technical language used in them and the distaste of the average official for statistics of any kind."

Statisticians and sociologist-actuaries do, at times, speak in language not fully understood by those in other disciplines. What they do in composing and testing prediction statistics does involve some heavy arithmetic. But actually the tables in Ohlin's *Selection for Parole* are not complex.

A public relations program is needed to overcome the indifference of parole boards and correctional workers toward prediction tables.

Tables should be developed to enable the paroling authority to determine the optimum time for release instead of merely predicting success or failure on parole (C-4; PB-1; P-1). As already pointed out, present tables do not show when a person is ready for release or whether he should be held for a longer time. Professor Herbert A. Bloch says:

> Predictive devices .... should be based upon the determination of factors pertaining to the optimum time for release and measurable criteria indicating responsiveness to treatment, rather than upon attempts to formulate criteria which may portend potential success or failure during the parole period.

Boards do not want to be bound by tables. Boards frequently want to reward prisoners who have taken advantage of the opportunities offered in prison. They believe parole is not a right but something that must be earned. They carefully study the inmate's record of achievement in prison, his efforts toward self-improvement, his changes in attitude, cooperation with the staff, relationships with fellow inmates, and any attitude of remorse he may have displayed. But, as one correctional worker points out, the incentive to gain freedom is so strong that prisoners go out of their way to behave well in institutions.

On the practical level, classification as a poor parole risk is stigmatic. Persons who are scored as potentially poor risks are at a disadvantage in their efforts not only to achieve parole, but also to make good on parole.

Legal restriction in some instances preclude the use of prediction statistics in parole selection. As Professor Norman S. Hayner points out in his informative article, "Why Do Parole Boards Lag in the Use of Prediction Scores?" intelligent parole selection often is made impossible because of legal or traditional restrictions. Among the legal impediments are the mandatory sentence, the requirement that a fixed portion of the sentence be served before a person is eligible for parole, and setting the minimum and maximum sentences so close together that few prisoners receive the benefit of parole supervision. These impediments, Hayner suggests, can be modified or removed. "Without changes in such laws or traditions," he declares, "a scientific aid like a prediction table is practically useless."

The results do not justify the costs (C-1; P-1). Computation of experience tables is a long, laborious, and expensive task. The question to be considered, one respondent says, is: How can we obtain maximum results for a particular job at a minimum cost?

There is general resistance to the actuarial approach. The cause of this resistance is more than merely a lack of familiarity with prediction statistics. It may be the ever present cultural lag in the social sciences, particularly in criminology and in the correctional field as a whole; it may be opposition to the introduction of rigid experimental and quantitative techniques into the social science field. Or it may be, as Michael Hakeem points out, the absence of any startling or dramatic demonstration of predictive capacity in the actuarial approach. When such a demonstration is made, he asserts, prediction will be used.

More research is needed. A large number of those who replied express the need for more research in prediction statistics. Several indicate the need to determine the extent to which the case study method or clinical study may determine success or failure on parole. Clinical studies, one suggest, can help to determine the prisoner's attitudes and motivations, and the personality problems which may obstruct his reformation. Another says it may be true that each case is a unique research study. "But," he adds, "we can't get away with just saying so. We have to start doing research to prove it. . . . Those advocating such an approach are obligated to find out how effective they can be."

APPENDIX

Sanford Bates

Formerly Director, Federal Bureau of Prisons and Commissioner, New York Board of Parole

After an experience of four years as parole commissioner for the State of New York I can say I believe prediction tables would have a definite value in the matter of parole selection. I do not conceive that any such prediction device can be so accurate as to justify any exclusive reliance on it. Individual judgment and study of each case is indispensable. The real value, and possibly the principal value of the prediction device, is that it reminds the person making the judgment of the importance of certain factors, and therefore its use might prevent disregarding or underweighing certain elements. Also, factors must be weighed to determine their influence and it would be risky to decide a case on the basis of the number of factors pro and con. One damaging negative factor might conceivably under special circumstances outweigh a dozen favorable ones. A formula based on the recorded experience of many cases is a valuable guide to a decision but it cannot supplant the neecessity for an intelligent, individual study of each instance.

HERBERT A. BLOCH
Professor of Sociology, Brooklyn College

Despite considerable shortcomings in the use of predictive devices in parole selection, I am still convinced they may serve a useful purpose in aiding parole boards and administrators in their deliberations. This is certainly not to say they may serve as a substitute for the careful consideration of each potential parolee. However, in a field in which parole judgments are so frequently made on the basis of expedience, serious errors in uncontrolled human insight, and the compilation of classification records which are woefully inadequate and imprecise—despite lip-service to progressive penology and science—the use of carefully conceived instruments should be extremely welcome. Predictive devices, however, should be based upon the determination of factors pertaining to the optimum time for release and measurable criteria indicating responsiveness to treatment, rather than upon attempts to formulate criteria which may portend potential success or failure during the parole period. Institutional and community conditions are too variable for us to develop an instrument at the present time of adequate reliability in respect to predictive tabulations of the latter type.

ROBERT G. CALDWELL
Professor of Criminology, University of Iowa

The present weaknesses of parole prediction tables have undoubtedly contributed to the reluctance of parole agencies to employ these tables. But perhaps more important has been the confusing categories and technical language used in them and the distaste of the average official for statistics of any kind. When the tables have been sufficiently refined they may provide an important instrument for parole agencies, but even if they are perfected—and there are reasons to believe that efforts to do this face almost insurmountable obstacles—it does not appear that they can ever replace a detailed investigation of each case. The most hardened criminal may have "gotten it out of his system" and become ready for parole despite his past record, and a young inmate may simply not be old enough to have a "bad record," even though he is a poor parole risk.

In short, each case is unique, and each person must be studied as an individual. Prediction tables may furnish clues, but there is now no reason to believe that tables will ever be efficient tools of selection if used alone. In fact, one may ask whether tables of any kind are necessary if carefully prepared case studies are made available, and whether prediction tables might not give parole agencies a false sense of proficiency and security, discouraging the use of case studies and causing officials to lose sight of the prisoner as a living and changing personality.

RUTH SHONLE CAVAN
Professor of Sociology, Rockford College

When prediction devices were first published, they seemed to hold great promise as an aid in selection of prisoners for parole. However, the devices are only partially predictive and therefore of limited use.

1. Only high or low scores have high predictive value. Prisoners with the middle range of scores are almost equally divided between those who are failures or successes on parole. Middle scores, therefore, are almost worthless for predictive purposes.

2. Even at the extremes of the scale, scores do not predict perfectly. For example, in Ohlin's scale, low scores −5 and −6 predict that 75 per cent of prisoners with these scores will become violators; 25 per cent will succeed on parole. At the high end of the scale prediction is more certain; with scores of 5 to 10, only 3 per cent will become violators.

3. Scores give only a probability of success. What any individual prisoner will do is unknown. For example, on Ohlin's scale there is no way to know which 25 per cent of prisoners with low scores will nevertheless succeed on parole.

4. A practical problem in constructing prediction scales is that few courts or prisons have the detailed data needed for good prediction.

5. The influence of postprison situations is not accounted for in prediction scales, which are nesessarily based on past situations and experiences. It may well be that past unfavorable factors may be offset by better parole supervision, better preparation of family and community for the return of the parolee, change of community, and so forth.

6. At best, the prediction scale is only one item in the information that a parole board needs. One may question whether the time involved in working out a prediction score for all pris-

oners is justified by the small number whose scores are even reasonably predictive.

7. However, the partial success would seem to justify additional research to determine what information is needed for better prediction and perhaps what weight should be given to past experience in relation to future situations after release.

RICHARD A. CHAPPELL
Chairman, U.S. Board of Parole

While I make no claim of experience in the use of prediction tables, I believe they have definite value if they are well devised. Courts and parole board members should be cautious in using prediction tables and not depend entirely upon them in reaching conclusions. If they are properly applied they can be useful in many cases and they offer a worthwhile area for further research and experimentation.

DONALD CLEMMER
Director, Department of Corrections District of Columbia

If I have one thought to offer it is that "by their prisonization shall ye know them." This is to say, in my judgment, that the conventional criteria customarily pondered in determining parole selection can have added value if authorities also have some judgment as to the depth to which the prison culture has penetrated the inmate personality. While this is subtle and intangible, it is important. The observable factors of institutional adjustment such as conduct, work record, schooling, and so on, need to be interpreted in the framework of the degree of prisonization in reference to the aging process. That it is complex to come to a judgment in prisonization goes without saying.

REED COZART
Pardon Attorney, U.S. Department of Justice

It is my feeling that prediction efforts will never be entirely successful. We can measure advantages, intelligence, education, family background, etc., but there has been no way found to measure or find out the intentions or the thinking of an individual. I have found through experience that we cannot predict the behavior of a prisoner upon release purely on the basis of his background and his institutional adjustment. I have personally failed miserably in both directions. Some who I thought had no chance made good; others failed miserably in the community after excellent institutional adjustment and a good prognosis.

HARRY C. DUPREE

Chairman, Army and Air Force Clemency and Parole Board

I do not believe the field of parole is ready at this time to undertake the use of prediction procedures. There are thirty or more parole boards on which members serve part time. Of the remaining twenty-five parole boards with which I am acquainted, it appears there are not many members who have accepted the claims of the specialists who devised the prediction tables that they could be used advantageously. These members, in my opinion, do not accept the somewhat automatic prediction in place of their individualized and personal appraisal as to the parolability of inmates.

Another problem is related to the staff and equipment which would be needed to build up and maintain the data upon which prediction tables would be based. Most parole officials are concerned in obtaining more parole officers, supervisors, and clerical help rather than in making attempts to hire staff to develop prediction services.

Finally, parole officials do not feel that any one system of developing prediction tables has achieved a level above other systems. Each system uses a different set of factors to arrive at its conclusions.

T. C. ESSELSTYN

Professor of Sociology, San Jose State College

1. I think it was Daniel Glaser who pointed out that every judgment is a statistical judgment. There is an element of mathematical chance or probability in almost every stand or determination, all formal and informal means of social control, i.e., the fact that we can predict within comfortable limits what the other fellow will do. When applied to parole, prediction devices make parole judgments more rational and more precise than they might be otherwise. I am not saying they are irrational or nonrational now. But it is always a rewarding thing to discover that

one's informed hunches and experienced conclusions square with mathematical facts.

2. Prediction devices and scores should never be used alone. Prediction instruments are an aid to judgment, not a substitute for judgment. And Norman Hayner has warned that prediction devices may involve a parole board in the problem of excess. That is, even though an inmate may be in a low score group, he may still be retained in prison if the probability of failure, however low, is still excessive; i.e., higher than that which the community ought reasonably be asked to bear.

3. In the same vein, it should be borne in mind that while the prediction device indicates probability of success or failure, the question before the parole board is: Should this inmate be paroled? Probable outcome on parole is only one of the many elements in a parole judgment and statisticians should never assume the contrary.

4. Prediction devices are of great value not alone for parole selection, but also as checks on institution programs and treatment practices. In California, all juvenile wards and practically all adult inmates (over 80 per cent) are released by way of parole, but prediction instruments are still used regardless of the near-universality of parole in this state. "Base expectancy scores" (i.e., probable parole outcome expressed as a percentage) are computed very early on both juvenile and adult wards and inmates in the two major systems, or will be computed when this plan is in full operation.

While I have a great many other views on prediction instruments, my vote must be cast in favor of their development and their use on a much more wide-spread plane than has been the case generally to date. Properly devised, prediction scores are powerful tools for all ranks in correction and for the taxpayer.

ARTHUR E. FINK
Dean, School of Social Work
University of North Carolina

I incline much more to the judgment of a judge who is wise, humane, and just than I do to the efficacy of prediction tables. The same applies to prison administrators—that they be wise, humane, and just. To me there is no substitute, mechanical or statistical, for human judgment and human feeling.

FRED FINSLEY
Chairman, California Adult Authority

I do not believe that, used alone, any mechanical prediction device is of material aid to a board member because it cannot record the subjective progress an individual has made. When one has gained considerable knowledge as to his problems and the contributing factors thereto, this information can be brought out only by skilled interviewing techniques. In some of our therapy and counseling programs, some individuals acquire a good deal of understanding as to their emotional difficulties; others learn a little, and some do not benefit at all. On the other hand, the mechanical predictive tables can sort out and place into categories an abundance of objective data which, if used in conjunction with skilled interviewing, can bring about much better results than either the subjective interview or the prediction table alone. The combined use of both methods can bring us much nearer to a scientific approach to sound parole release procedures.

VERNON FOX
Chairman, Criminology and Corrections
Florida State University

I suspect that parole prediction, per se, is not much used outside Illinois. The factors used are generally historical factors, concerning work habits, geographic stability, marital stability, age, and the other background factors generally accumulated prior to incarceration. On the basis of these factors, approximately 80 per cent are successful on parole. This means that one-fifth may be denied parole on the basis of background factors.

Behind any human behavior is a mass of factors which, I suppose, could be coded and punched on cards. They would have to be divided into "predisposing" factors and "precipitating" factors. All the factors in parole prediction charts are predisposing factors. In predicting any behavior, one has to ask two questions: (1) How stressful is the situation? (2) How stable is the personality bearing that stress? A more flexible and, if a competent board is doing it, a better job can result from an examination and evaluation of each case on the basis of the predisposing and precipitating factors affecting it than can be done by a punch card system or prediction chart in which the background factors for the past thirty years are compiled to project the probability of an individual under consideration for parole in a specific setting.

Parole prediction offers excellent research possibilities and provides information which should be used as background material. Like the group tests of personality, a standardized measure can be considered to be reliable and valid when used in groups because the varieties of errors neutralize each other. Both are dangerous when conclusions are drawn from them which affect the treatment of a specific individual without professional evaluation of the individual in his specific setting.

HOWARD B. GILL
Director, Institute of Correctional Administration,
American University

Prediction is, of course, the final goal of any scientific endeavor and is essential in any analysis which lays claim to being scientific. Thus the claim of some so-called social scientists that "the facts must speak for themselves" and that "value judgments are to be avoided" is a display either of an inability to come to a conclusion or a lack of courage to stick one's neck out.

However, the same cannot be said of prediction formulae in parole selection, which have engaged the attention of criminological research during the past twenty-five or thirty years to the exclusion of more significant operational research. There have been three major pitfalls in the development of prediction formulae: First, the reliance on a single criterion of success in the rehabilitation of prisoners; namely, recidivism. Secondly, the attempt to select certain characteristics per se as indicative of success or failure on parole. And finally, the attempt to substitute a static formula for clinical insight.

Although recidivism is the most obvious measure of success in prison work, because it is subject to so many intervening variables it is also the most unreliable. Nevertheless, in order to produce a quick and easy method of insuring popular approval in parole selection, base expectancy analyses have been developed which classify offenders according to risk of recidivism. Thus the vagaries of parole supervision rather than change in criminal tendencies based on individual treatment determine parole selection. This is a superficial oversimplification.

Again, to attempt to select certain specific characteristics which appear to correlate with "success on parole" (i.e., non-recidivism) is to fail to see that it is not the possession of such characteristics in themselves (which may be common to many people, prisoners and otherwise) but rather the degree of imbalance in any characteristic which may result in success or failure. Such imbalance cannot be attached to any particular set of characteristics and cannot be generalized to fit into a formula. Only clinical insight can interpret and predict, and formulae based on statistical correlations are no substitute for clinical insight.

Finally, the most unfortunate result of this concern with prediction formulae in parole selection lies in its influence on the direction and content of research in the field of criminology. More than anything else this preoccupation with prediction formulae has kept criminological research on an academic level and blocked more useful operational research.

Correction today could stand a moratorium on research which seeks a quick and easy formula for prediction in order to avoid the risk of possible failure in parole selection. Screening tests and prediction tables are poor substitutes for the courage of exploration and new discovery. Chi-squares and correlations are all right in their place; but they can never replace the spirit and the vitality essential for finding new operational frontiers. Despite the number of impressive and expensive prediction studies published during the past twenty-five or thirty years and the exaggerated claims of some of their proponents, most of these studies have produced results of little operational value.

SHELDON GLUECK
Professor, Harvard Law School

A major weakness in the administration of criminal justice is the fact that while "individualization" is necessary, it must depend largely on "hunch." True, administrators of parole try, conscientiously, to weigh the pros and cons of each case, doing so more and more on the basis of a case history. True, further, such officials gradually develop an art of fairly acceptable discrimination between cases, for in making parole decisions, as in all walks of life, practical experience is valuable. Nevertheless, there is a crucial missing ingredient; namely, an instrument which will enable the administrator to bring to bear on the instant case the systematically arranged precipitate of past experience with hundreds of other cases. It is this that the well-organized prediction table supplies.

It needs to be emphasized, because it is so often overlooked by critics, that the creators of prediction devices (not only for parole selection, but also for sentencing and for early identification of prospective delinquents) do not urge that such tables be applied in any mechanical, routine fashion; they are adjuncts to both the individual case history and individual experience of the parole board member. Tables can never replace brains; and the administrator who finds the prediction-device indication to spell out a high probability of success on parole and during a reasonable period thereafter for the parole applicant under consideration, but also finds other indications that raise a question mark in that particular instance is, of course, free to deal contrary to the actuarial indications.

Every few years prediction tables should be renovated by a systematic checkup on their actual effectiveness because both correctional facilities and community aid to paroles undergo change with time.

Of course prediction devices need to be improved. But the fact that they are not perfect is no reason for certain critics to assume a pose of petulant disdain; at least not until they produce a better device in aid of parole selection.

KEITH S. GRIFFITHS
Chief of Research, California Youth Authority

In the California Youth Authority we have developed what we call a "base expectancy" or "prediction" instrument which has made possible a classification of wards based upon the likelihood of their violating or not violating their parole within specified periods of their exposure. This instrument was developed by relating available measurements of the ward (prior record, age, type of offense, and so on) to parole performance and combining these measures through multiple correlational analysis into a single score or category which maximally predicts parole performance. In our estimation, such an instrument has two important uses.

One use is to equate populations for the evaluation of treatment effects. For example, we have the problem of trying to evaluate the variation in violation rates of wards released from our different institutions and camps. We found a considerable variation between these rates and wanted to determine whether these differences were the result of the kind of wards treated or were due to some other factor.

A recent analysis showed that the violation rate of the releasees of most institutions was satisfactorily explained by the base expectancy classification of the youths released. However, the releasees from our two reception centers and from our forestry camps did significantly better than expected. It is not possible to explain why those released from reception centers and camps performed better on parole than expected. However, these findings present us with important leads which suggest that early release from a reception center or from forestry camp training produces better-than-average results.

The base expectancy classification also offers utility as a screening device for selecting candidates for early release. Recently, we placed into operation a plan to compute the base expectancy score of each admission to our reception centers. The parole risk classification into which the individual falls is presented to the Youth Authority Board. This score is considered along with many other yardsticks in determining whether the individual should be assigned to an early release program. If used judiciously, this instrument offers the promise of important savings through the reduction of the length of stay of offenders who do not require periods of institutional care.

GUS HARRISON
Director, Michigan Department of Corrections

I do not believe that anyone who is well acquainted with parole prediction devices makes any wild claims for them. From what I have heard and read of prediction devices, I believe the "smart" position of those in the know is that there is a great deal of promise in the use of simple predictive devices. There is good reason to justify experimental application in identifying those who will succeed or fail on parole.

I am not satisfied that all of the objections to prediction devices are valid. On the other hand, I am not satisfied that all of those objections have been washed out. In my opinion, prediction tables need to be tested periodically with a view to their improvement.

There are still many unanswered problems. However, it is gratifying to note that competent research on many of these problems is in process. I conclude that on the basis of already existing evidence, the predictive approach in the field of parole selection looks like it can do the job of eliminating much of the often observed guesswork, speculation, and emotional excursions dealing with the selection of parolees.

NORMAN S. HAYNER
Professor of Sociology, University of Washington, and formerly Chairman, Washington Board of Prison Terms and Paroles

As the sociologists see it, prediction scores not only can but should be used as scientific aids in making parole decisions. Some of the major objections by parole board members to the use of prediction devices in parole selection may be met, in part, through (1) modification of legal and traditional impediments to intelligent selection for parole; (2) an honest and continuing program of public relations within a given jurisdiction in order to change the social climate of that area, thus making the use of prediction tables and other scientific devices more acceptable; (3) increasing recognition by parole boards of a shift in the correctional field from a primary concern with the individual offender to the constructive use of groups, thus supplementing their emphasis on the individual case; and (4) improvement by sociologists of the technique of parole prediction by such devices as developing a more satisfactory theoretical basis, refining the methods of measurement, and including terms related to prison adjustment.

FREDERICK A. C. HOEFER
Formerly Alternate Chairman, Army and Air Force Clemency and Parole Board

When we approach the question to what extent arithmetical prediction devices should be used in parole administration, a considerable degree of caution seems advisable. First of all, there are certain limitations to all predictions that are based on statistical research. What is predictable is not the certainty of a future event in a particular case, but merely the odds for or against such an event. In terms of parole prediction, what can be ascertained is a "chance" of success, based on a group of similar cases in which certain significant factors are believed to have been identical.

Secondly, and more important, prediction devices should never be used as a mechanical substitute for individual case study. This is particularly true when we make a decision granting or denying parole. A strong warning is in order against any attempt to substitute arithmetic for judgment when making a decision concerning a human life. Individual case study by trained professional workers is the only possible basis for both decisions. It may be suggested here that the case analyst, after completing his study and evaluation of the case, could use a prediction table as a control device to check his own thinking and to see whether he has overlooked an important element in the case. To that extent, the use of a prediction device could be defended. It should be used only by a professionally trained case analyst and only for control purposes.

Thirdly, I have to mention the parole risk, as such, is not the only factor to be considered when making a parole decision. In this connection, there is a growing belief among correctional workers that many "doubtful risk" cases ought to be paroled because it is better to supervise such individuals than to release them at a later date without any strings attached. On the other hand, it is sometimes impossible to release a relatively good risk where the parolee's one-time crime was of a heinous type and has received much unfavorable publicity. In such a case the community at large may be unwilling to accept his release on parole. Unfortunate as this may be, no parole administrator will ever be able to ignore strong community sentiment in such cases.

ARTHUR V. HUFFMAN
State Criminologist Illinois Department of Public Safety

Since 1933 the Illinois Parole and Pardon Board has used a prediction report prepared by sociologists—carrying the payroll title of sociologists-actuary—for each prisoner considered for parole. The final part of each of these reports consists of the sentence: "This inmate is in a class in which ——— per cent may be expected to violate the parole agreement."

Parole Board members use this as an aid in the selection of prisoners for parole, along with other aids such as the sociological, psychological, or psychiatric reports prepared by the criminologist's professional staff. Thus, the prediction report is a supplement to professional, clinical judgment, since it provides a benchmark based on the statistics of general parole violation against which the personal impressions and professional reports can be weighed.

Like any statistical device, these prediction tables have their limitations. Historically, they are part of the growing empirical social science of the twentieth century. Conceptually, the Illinois tables are designed for the specific purpose of selection for parole, and differ from the work of such researchers as Sheldon and Eleanor Glueck. Empirically, the actuaries have not been able to adequately utilize certain types of data (such as psychological data from individual questionnaires), and since the Illinois experience tables are based on parolees, the hypothetical violation rates among those not paroled are matters of conjecture.

The experience or prediction table for parole violation can be viewed as an analogy of the common life insurance table and an oversimplified, but reasonable explanation is as follows: Statistical data are accumulated on a group of prisoners who have been paroled, and the total number of this group who violate is calculated as a percentage of the entire group. Then, some single item of information is broken up into categories, and each category has its violation percentage calculated. If much lower than average, it is scored as a favorable factor; if around the average, it is scored as a neutral factor; if much higher than average, it is scored as an unfavorable factor.

It is my own belief that we need to recognize the increasing significance and the potentiality of the statistical approach in correction, and I fully share the thinking expressed recently by Dr. J. P. Shalloo in his letter to me wherein he put it thus: "We might even suggest computers or electronic historicometers in conjunction with futurometers and we could all sit back and let the vibrations take over to warn and predict. Sounds fantastic? Well, the whole mechanical trend is just that. Prisoners were once numbers. Now they may become holes in a card, and so will their relatives."

GEORGE G. KILLINGER
Professor of Criminology and Corrections
Florida State University
Formerly Chairman, U.S. Board of Parole

Prediction scales should be administered as a routine pre-parole procedure. Their use is warranted if they do nothing more than make a board of parole look twice at their selection methods and parole decisions. Even if the final objective or subjective decision of the board is contrary to the prognostication of the tabular scale, the board will have given sufficient study and analysis to the case to be sure that they can defend their final parole action.

While selection procedures have generally improved during recent years, we can all remember when understaffed boards of parole were making selections in great numbers, in very short periods of time, and based upon cursory reviews of inadequate diagnostic material. I am often reminded of the prisoner who had anticipated his parole eligibility for ten years and, upon returning from his brief interview with the parole judge, stated: "I didn't expect to make parole on the first go-around, but what gets me is the fact that the interviewing judge didn't know one thing about me." Parole boards have often known too little about the prospective parolee, and any procedure that will help present and future boards arrive at the real worth of the individual, whether through clinical material, interviews by entire boards sitting en banc, comprehensive institutional progress reports, evidence of contrition, family and community interest—or prediction scores—should be encouraged. We must get away from fast, subjective selections. This can best be brought about through the combination of objective decisions by a sufficient number of properly trained parole board members.

JOSEPH D. LOHMAN
Dean, School of Criminology
University of California

In regard to your question about "The Present Status of Parole Prediction in Parole Selection," I can only say that in Illinois the system has remained almost dormant during the past eight years. This stems largely from an absence of knowledge and understanding of the meaning and significance of parole prediction tables and scores. In Illinois we had come to a practice in which the tables were utilized as a check or measuring stick by means of which we could assess Parole Board actions both collectively and in individual cases. That is to say , if the decision of the Board, either affirmative or negative, was at odds with the probable score as to success or failure, then the Board was prepared to specify more clearly particular grounds on which the parole was granted or denied. Under these conditions, such tables were in no sense a substitute for Board action; nevertheless, they afforded an important caution against irresponsible or subjective action by the Parole Board. The employment of prediction methods should be more carefully developed than has usually been the case. It was with such considerations in mind that I insisted the program be developed during my administration of the Illinois Parole and Pardon Board. Our success in driving the violation rate to an all-time low attests to the validity of such considerations. The prediction tables are of inestimable value; unfortunately their meaning and application are generally misunderstood.

HARVEY L. LONG
Executive Secretary
Illinois Youth Commission

I have had no experience specifically in the use of "prediction devices" as tools employed in the parole selection process. At most, when used with adults, the procedures of prediction merely supplemented the clinical summation. At one time in Illinois the so-called prediction process was used to classify the total number of cases paroled as to percentage of various risk categories. As I recall, it was the hope to keep the high risk cases within reasonable proportions as related to the immediate social and economic conditions and the current success or failure experience of present parolees. The percentage of higher risk cases could go up or down, depending on the climate. The "prediction device" was thought to be helpful, although I know of no attempts to validate its use statistically.

The general concepts growing out of the "prediction studies" seem to me to be of great value. It is unfortunate that we have tied them to the word "prediction." I would rather consider them as check-list items to be used in the regular casework process, and, therefore, to be related to the clinical summation.

Frank Loveland
Formerly Assistant Director
Federal Bureau of Prisons

In the field of correction we have had too little pertinent information upon which to base decisions. One of the most important decisions has to do with parole selection. There are two types of pertinent information to be considered in this decision; first, that having to do with the individual himself and the progress he has made under treatment, and second, the experiences of persons of similar backgrounds after their release into the community. When a parole board member weighs the pros and cons of a case, he is, in effect, calling upon his past experience to tell him whether a person of this type will succeed or fail. The prediction scale attempts to do the same job but in a much more systematic and scientific manner. This does not mean that I believe a calculation based upon a few factors can take the place of a wise person's analysis of a complete diagnostic history and a report of the individual's reaction to the institutional program. The claim that it can has done a disservice to prediction scales.

If I were a parole board member, I would want a predictability scale and a score on each applicant. But I would want it not to make my decision for me, but to check with my appraisal of the entire individual. I would recognize, also, that predictability scales generally have given little or no attention to the effects of the treatment program in the institution or to the quality of parole supervision in the community. Are we to assume that what happens to a man in the institution and the type of supervision he receives on parole have nothing to do with whether he succeeds or fails? Any intelligent selection procedure takes these factors into account.

Ben Meeker
Chief Probation Officer
U.S. District Court, Chicago

The concept of prediction in parole selection has too often been geared to an actuarial cataloging and weighing of objective factors in the background of the individual. This has greatly handicapped the utility of most prediction instruments, since actuarial tables cannot be designed for application in individual situations. No doubt there are valuable statistical studies of the recovery rates of hospital patients, but I know of no physicians who seriously attempt to evaluate prognosis of individual patients by actuarial methods. For statistical and research purposes and if used primarily to measure general trends in the efficiency or inefficiency of more subjective methods of parole selection, such devices have value.

Efforts to predict outcome are, of course, inherent in selection for parole, but valid prediction must be based upon subjective as well as objective factors. To rely solely on objective prediction is to revert to a deterministic philosophy of life which ignores the whole concept of potential for rehabilitation and change.

Predictive selection must, therefore, include such essentially subjective factors as the individual's current set of values, his sense of purpose, and some assessment of attitude changes which may have occurred in confinement.

Although systematically identified objective factors belong in a program of parole selection, they can only complement the subjective evaluation of social, psychological, and emotional factors in the personality of the individual. All subjective and objective factors must then be related to any new potentials in the individual's prospective economic or social situation. Among such potentials are the skills of professionally competent parole officers and the dynamic of a constructive relationship between the parolee and his parole counselor.

Austin H. MacCormick
Executive Director, Osborne Association

I believe in the potential value of parole prediction devices, particularly those of the "table of factors" type, when they are developed scientifically and used wisely. I expect their usefulness to increase as statistical compilations, prerelease and postrelease case histories, and research provide more and more of the data needed to validate predictions.

On the other hand, I recognize the weaknesses inherent in even the best prediction devices available today. One is that, even if they can predict with reasonable accuracy what percentage of 1,000 consecutive parolees will succeed or fail, they cannot with the same accuracy predict what will happen to Prisoner X, the individual under consideration by the board.

Another weakness is that prediction devices list, weigh, and designate, as favorable or unfavorable, factors in the prospective parolee's past and present life history, with some projections into the future but no certainty that significant factors will not change for better or worse after the prisoner is paroled. For example, an unexpected, severe, and prolonged increase in unemployment in the area to which a parolee is released may outweigh a half-dozen favorable factors.

Finally, prediction devices cannot be considered universally applicable. They must be—but seldom are—varied for different regions, states, institutions, and periods of time, and revised as major social and economic changes take place in areas where parolees are living and working.

If parole board members keep all these weaknesses in mind and consider the prediction device only one of the many sources of information on the individual parole prospect which they should utilize, it can be a safe and useful tool. Its use may cause the members to give proper consideration to factors which they would otherwise slight or disregard wholly. For the new and inexperienced board member especially, a prediction device of the table type provides a convenient list of factors which research indicates to be favorable or unfavorable to parole success.

RUSSELL G. OSWALD
Chairman, New York State Board of Parole

If we had prediction devices which were based on scientifically obtained data and which took into account not only the individual's personality makeup and his personal, social, and criminal history, but also his overall response to correctional treatment and the optimal time for release, I would be in favor of using such predictive devices as a tool selecting individuals for parole.

In New York State Division of Parole we know from our own research studies that certain groups of parolees will prove to be better parole risks than other groups. We also know that in the better groups there will be many individual failures and in the poorer groups there will be many individual successes. Aside from the obvious limitations of a strictly actuarial approach in the profession of rehabilitating persons, there are always other considerations which demand that the paroling authority rely on its own evaluation of each individual. Among the other considerations are the nature of the crime, the adequacy of the parole program, the kind of parole supervision available, and, finally and most importantly, the conviction of professional parole practitioners that the parole of any person is a matter requiring individualized consideration.

C. TERENCE PIHLBLAD
Professor of Sociology, University of Missouri

In general, I would favor prediction techniques as a supplement to other information in making decisions with respect to granting or denying parole. I know that expectancy tables have their definite limitations from both a theoretical and technical point of view. To date, they do not take account of the time factor—that is, the problem of advisability of holding a subject for a longer period of time; they do not provide the cut-off point below which one would wish to deny parole; they cannot take into account the relative effectiveness of supervision under different parole systems. It has been suggested by some authorities that they may be used by some parole boards as a rationalization for limiting parole to a relatively few cases. (In Missouri, for example, where only about 30 per cent of all releases are by parole, this might readily be the case.) I could see also that some lay boards, made up as ours is of former police officers, with no technical background or training, could be impressed with statistical hocus pocus and make the administration of parole almost purely a mechanical business. Prediction could well supply them with the "scientific" magic which would solve problems for them.

In spite of these limitations, however, I believe that expectancy tables, properly interpreted by competent personnel, and in spite of their limited prediction success, could have value as a guide and as supplementary to other kinds of material in parole administration. It seems to me that there would be at least two advantages. One would be to serve as a guide or indicator in reaching the decision. The second would be to indicate the kinds of subjects who appear to need intensive supervision as distinguished from those who appear to be able to operate largely on their own and need less guidance or assistance. There might then be a more economical distribution of staff time and effort that seems to prevail at the present.

GEORGE J. REED
Member, U.S. Board of Parole

In recent years a number of criminologists and researchers in the field of criminal behavior have been intrigued with the development of prediction tables and other such devices. These studies and prediction tables provide one of a number of techniques and resource information which should be a part of the experience and knowledge of every competent parole board member. The study of human behavior, and especially criminal behavior, is not an exact science and cannot be adequately measured solely in a table or chart when attempting to reach a final decision on a specific parole applicant.

Prediction tables that have been documented on a sufficiently large number of cases which comprise a variety of socioeconomic settings provide an excellent frame of reference of comparison for a parole board to gauge research studies of their own local experiences. Thus, when a parole board staff has, over a period of time, compiled detailed information on their own experiences, these tentative findings can, with benefit, be compared with other more comprehensive studies and prediction tables. The board is, therefore, in a position to arrive at conclusions regarding their own program having validity and meaning as it is compared with broader experiences.

Well-informed parole board members should be kept currently advised through staff research on where they have failed and where they have succeeded in selecting parole releasees. Thus, the parole board member, faced with the grave responsibility of making a decision that affects the life of the prisoner, his family, and possibly society itself, has a wealth of source material, both local and national, upon which to rely in arriving at a final judgment.

SOL RUBIN
Counsel, National Council on Crime and Delinquency

The concept of prediction, the very use of the term "prediction," is in contradiction to all experience in human affairs. One can as sensibly try to predict the course of history of nations and cultures as to predict, in any detail, the course of history of an individual. The unknowns are infinite; the element of chance exists always. While generalizations about historical developments and the patterns of the future of individuals can be hazarded, the kind of pinpointing that says individual A will be a delinquent in five years or individual B will or will not violate his parole is something that is obviously speculative. My impression is that prediction devices have lost much of their appeal and glamor.

However, the approach of diagnosis is quite another matter. We have vast experience in the study of individuals and their behavior on parole and in other situations. Certainly it is the part of wisdom to examine these histories with great care, to learn how to classify individuals in particular situations in terms of a diagnostic approach for the application of the most appropriate treatment or planning. We do not then predict their behavior but closely attend the course of development of the individual in the new situation and are ready to adjust the treatment process or otherwise act in the light of developments. This is quite different from the concept of the prediction tables.

THORSTEN SELLIN
Professor of Sociology, University of Pennsylvania

Authorities responsible for parole have a duty to protect the community insofar as they are able to do so by releasing on parole those prisoners who are least likely to recidivate. Experience has shown that the risk of recidivism depends on many factors in the life history of prisoners. Neither intuition nor "common sense" can evaluate these factors adequately; they can be disclosed by research that seeks to correlate them with the degree of adjustment on parole. It is such research that has led to the development of actuarial, experience, or "prediction" tables of which those in use in Illinois furnish an example. Parole boards should consider it imperative to construct similar instruments as aids in parole selection, even though it is understood they cannot be consistently applied because of limitations inherent in the criminal law and the sentencing practices of the courts or imposed by considerations that, in the balance, are weightier than the risk of recidivism.

L. B. STEPHENS
Executive Director
Alabama Board of Pardons and Paroles

The parole process presupposes two primary functions; namely, parole selection and treatment. The success of the treatment process depends to a large degree upon the proper selection of those to receive the treatment. Selection of those to be granted parole in many jurisdictions is done without sufficient case materials and by board members who are not trained in the correction field. In selecting candidates for parole we strive to increase the number of paroles granted to prisoners who are likely to succeed on parole and likewise to reduce the number granted to those who are likely to fail. In this process a well worked out prediction device for the area of the operation is important, helpful, and significant.

In the use of any prediction device it is important to know the purpose it is intended to serve and its limitations. A prediction table to be valid must be prepared by personnel who are adequately trained to organize work, conduct interviews, prepare reports, and carry on the research necessary to the development of prediction methods.

The prediction table will not serve its best and intended purpose when it is used alone. It can, however, become an important adjunct in the parole selection process when supplemented by other well-established sources of information as a well-prepared presentence investigation report, classification and progress reports, institutional reports, and reactions of interested persons.

PAUL W. TAPPAN
Professor, School of Law New York University
Formerly Chairman, U.S. Board of Parole

It seems apparent, from the parole prediction research that has been done thus far, that it is now possible to determine with some accuracy the probabilities of success and failure of a prisoner as he is released under supervision. This is surely useful, both as a matter of evaluating the relationship of particular prediction criteria to success and also as a device to assist parole boards in making release decisions. It seems to me, however, that prediction formulae should not be used mechanically to determine eligibility for parole. This is so, in part, because a large proportion of cases lie in the middle range and the unfortunate tendency might be to exclude many cases that could do well on release.

I am critical of the criteria employed in most of the parole studies because they relate so little to the quality of the offender's experience during correctional treatment, both in prison and under supervision. Since most prisoners must return to the community and ideally should do so under parole supervision, it is clearly desirable that prediction instruments should be developed to determine the optimum time of release rather than merely risk of failure without regard to the time of release. It is also true, I believe, that the prediction studies have given insufficient attention to the question of the seriousness of the offenses that the prisoner has committed in the past and may commit in the future. Surely it is important to know not only the likelihood of his getting into trouble again, but how serious his infractions may be if he is paroled.

Finally, if a prediction table is to be used in parole, it must be continuously revised so as to reflect the changing circumstances which bear upon the probabilities of the success of prisoners when they are released.

NEGLEY K. TEETERS
Professor of Sociology, Temple University

Parole prediction devices, like intelligence and aptitude tests, are worthy attempts to be more objective regarding potential adjustment or success in later life. Any technique or philosophy that modifies or replaces mere hunches in predicting success on parole is desirable. However, as prediction charts are confusing so far as categories are concerned, they are not likely to be accepted by traditional parole officials. Other limitations of such charts are, first, the problem of weighing each factor as a liability or an asset; and second, possible ambiguity in classification—for instance, what is "socially inadequate or a "ne 'er-do-well"? How "socially inadequate" or 'industrious" is the candidate?

Another serious limitation of mechanical parole techniques is that the parole petitioner is a person, not a mere digit, and this presents a hazard of losing sight of him as a living personality. Prediction charts nullify that indefinable, yet precious quality some parole officers may have which we call insight, a quality that must be accepted in any human interaction.

Objective research must be continued in parole prediction charts but they must be used cautiously and wisely. In this respect they fall into the same category as intelligence tests—to be used as guides but not to be followed blindly.

GEORGE B. VOLD
Professor of Sociology University of Minnesota

The simple fact is well recognized that some inmates are much better parole risks than others. Prediction devices express aspects of this differential risk in terms of statistical probability. As such they provide a firm, objective basis for the exercise of administrative judgment on what action should be taken in connection with each case.

More than thirty years ago, when I first presented the results of my own parole prediction study to a state conference of social work and outlined some possibilities for its utilization in practice, I was attacked by local parole authorities and others for trying to substitute a mechanical device—a prediction table—for the wise and humane judgment of an experienced parole administrator.

So far as I can judge, many parole authorities still react in much the same way: they do not want their judgments about human character hampered by the restrictions of prediction devices. The objection, of course, is as absurd now as it was thirty years ago. No one would argue that the fever thermometer, the electrocardiograph, or the x-ray machine substitutes for the doctor's judgment in diagnosis. These devices simply give some objective basis on which the doctor may anchor his judgments about desirable treatment. Parole prediction devices should be understood in the same manner.

Intelligent parole selection needs similar objective anchorage in terms of firm information about the statistical probabilities of success or failure involved with reference to each candidate for parole. There should be more, not less, use of predictive devices. As parole authorities become better trained in the utilization of objective prediction devices, one may expect improvement in the exercise of administrative judgment in parole selection.

WALTER M. WALLACK
Warden, Walkill Prison, New York

From what I know about the method of deriving prediction formulae, I have no confidence in their reliability as an instrument for determining whether an individual should be paroled. There are too many intangibiles involved. Some of the factors taken into account cannot be reduced to objectivity. Currently we must depend upon the judgment of individuals who are intelligent, familiar with all the factors involved in criminality from beginning to end, and with the so-called correctional process as it may be applied in a given jurisdiction—a process which might not even be correctional in some jurisdictions.

The total experience and common-sense judgment of paroling officials is more reliable, it seems to me, than any formula based on mathematical probability. This is not to say that sometime in the future it will not be possible to find some significant assistance in forming a judgment as to whether or not to parole by means of one of these newfangled, terrifically expensive 'thinking machines." If these electronic machines, as a result of feeding a great amount of data, can be useful in the physical sciences, one might dare to believe they would have some value in arriving at possible human conduct outcomes. I believe, however, it will be a long time in the future before such machines can or will be used. In any event, I think it will always be necessary for one or more human beings to dominate in the judgment as to what might be expected in the conduct of any member of the human race.

I believe that the largest single reason for this is the infinite number of differences among individual members of the race. I wish it were possible to predict human conduct with a highly reliable degree of accuracy. For the present and for some time to come it seems that we will have to depend upon the expert judgment of one or more individuals with reference to another. No two conduct patterns are ever developed in exactly the same way. Heredity and environmental pressures always result in a unique outcome in the development of individual human conduct. In my opinion, no Utopia is in sight. We must depend upon the best possible judgments even though these may fall far short of perfection. We can only strive to narrow the margin of error, which does and always will persist in the judgment of one human being over another.

14

IT'S TIME TO START COUNTING*

EXPERIENCE IS NOT ENOUGH

N<small>OT TOO LONG AGO</small>, medical men "knew from experience" that "bleeding" sick people was good for them. Medical men also "knew enough from experience" not to prescribe tomatoes for one's diet. Neither of these "knowns" had been obtained from systematic study; rather they were the kinds of folklore "knowns" that had arisen from chance experience: physicians had seen sick people get well who had had their blood let; they had not fed tomatoes to many people who did not get sick.

Rightfully, present-day management training courses stress that experience is not enough. They teach that when someone says he has eighteen years' experience, you should ask him whether he means eighteen years' experience or one year's experience eighteen times.

At the turn of the century, a psychologist ran a series of experiments to test the premise that experience at a task necessarily brings improvement in performance. Taking the game of darts, he drew a line fifteen feet from the target on the wall. The subjects were given darts and told to stand behind the line and try to hit the target. However, the psychologist added another condition to the game: he placed an opaque curtain, from the floor to above eye level, between the subject and the target. Subject had to toss the dart over the curtain into a target they could not see. Perhaps even more important, they could not see how close they came to the target at each throw. No matter how many times they threw the darts, ignorance of results prevented them from improving their ability to hit the target.

Nonsensical, you say. Of course experience is useless if one does not know where the target (goal) is or how close are one's throws. Yet, much of our experience in the correctional field is exactly like this. How much do we agree on our correctional goals?

*J. Douglas Grant: *National Council on Crime and Delinquency Journal*, 8:259-264, July, 1962.

How many of us receive feedback on how well we are doing in achieving our goals? Can we make explicit what we expect and then compare what actually happens with what we expected to happen?

That experience is not enough has been dramatically demonstrated by Hakeem. He presented the case summaries of 200 former parolees to experienced professional parole agents and asked them to classify these summaries into successes and failures. He then asked a group of accountants to do the same. The agents did slightly worse than the accountants and neither did better than chance. In addition, there was a systematic bias. While the records had been evenly divided between successes and failures, the parole agent classified too many as failures, markedly reducing the possibility of accurate prediction.

An associate superintendent of the California Department of Corrections recently put some of *his* years of experience to the test. (He should be commended. This is the only way to separate truth from fantasy.) He interviewed 283 inmates just prior to their release on parole and made predictions concerning their likelihood of success. In addition, he reviewed psychiatric case histories and made further predictions on the basis of this material. The result was that his interview predictions correlated .20 with parole outcome; his predictions based on interview *plus* clinical information correlated .21. A base expectancy formula developed two years previously, however, correlated .48 with the parole outcome. Even when combined with the interview and clinical record judgments, the base expectancy formula was not markedly improved; the multiple correlation was still .48. Conclusion: This administrator's wealth of experience was much less effective in predicting parole performance than was systematic study of one year's experience. Further, with much more information, the experienced professional was unable to add anything to improve the predictions derived from systematic study.

TOO MUCH MONEY FOR TOO LITTLE RETURN

Thirty years ago Adolf Meyer suggested that social agencies could get closer to their clients by trying to understand the whole person. He proposed case histories as a way of doing this. But, as with many good ideas, the case history method has become distorted. Often, workers in social agencies are so busy collecting, completing, and filing case histories that they have little time left for their clients. Further, the case history records often become so voluminous that they can be used only superficially, if at all, in making decisions affecting the clients.

Vinter and Janowitz conducted an organizational study of seven older-youth correctional institutions. One of their major findings was that the institutions had far more information on their inmates than they were able to use. Many decisions concerning program changes and inmate management were constantly being made, but the voluminous information files seldom had any effect upon these decisions.

Correctional agencies, like other social agencies, have two main concerns: keeping case records and making decisions. Both represent tremendous expenditures of time and money, but the two activities have little influence on each other. The information-collectors are busy describing the whole person. The decision-makers are busy trying to cope with a multitude of pressures in a field where little systematic study or body of facts is available. This lack of integration does not imply that management is unconcerned with facts, but rather that no adequate means of bringing the two together has yet been devised.

Leslie Wilkins, however, has shown how prediction procedures can help management to state what it expects from known information and to study systematically the ways of bringing about variations from the expected.

PREDICTION DEVICES HOLD UP

A formula based on one year's releases to parole will predict parole success for subsequent years. The California Department of Corrections has tested this out by using various formulas in several studies over a number of years.

In a study of parole caseload size, a base expectancy formula predicted releases for 1957 and 1958 as well as it did for its original cross-validation sample in 1956. The studies discussed previously, in which interview-derived predictions were compared with formula-derived predictions, showed that a formula predicted parole releases better than it predicted its original cross-validation sample.

These validations held up when analyzed by quarter year, geographic region to which paroled, and institution from which released. In addition, they held up for both arrest and recommitment criteria.

Base expectancies developed for women parolees during the three years ending in June, 1958, also held up for women released to parole in '59 and '60.

A very promising development is Gottfredson's effort to predict actual Parole Board decisions. It appears that parole boards are more predictable than parolees. From intake information such as severity of offense, prior incarceration, minimum eligible parole date, and age, Gottfredson is able to predict the Parole Board's decisions in setting institution time and parole time. He found that correlations between predicted time and actual time set by the Board were greater than .60.

While cross-validations have yet to be made, these findings are most encouraging. They form the basis for a study, sponsored by the National Institute of Mental Health, of decision made by the Adult Authority and California's Board of Trustees for Women. Discrepancies between formula predictions and actual decisions will be studied for additional relevant information.

Gottferdson's data suggest that the Parole Board was not setting terms on the basis of case history information known to predict parole success. Even when the Parole Board's decisions were studied separately for each offense group, there was almost no relationship between an inmate's base expectancy score and the institution or parole time he actually served. Since this study, the base expectancy scores have been made available to the paroling authority.

PROGRAMS HELP SOME, MAY HARM OTHERS

Intensive psychiatric casework was given institutionalized older wards of the California Youth Authority. Before treatment, these wards had been divided into amenables and nonamenables. Both groups were matched with controls who did not receive treatment. The first 100 amenables released from treatment and institutionalization had a total of only 206 months reconfinement, compared with the 480 months for the first 100 control amenables released.

This difference was based on a 33-month follow-up. More important, perhaps, is the finding that the treated nonamenables had 550 months of reconfinement while the *control* nonamenables had only 481. These latter negative effects of treatment on particular types of inmates, though not statistically significant, are similar to the results of other studies.

The Navy has experimented with a therapeutic community type of program for its confinees, in which subjects were divided into high and low social maturity classifications and members of the community supervisory staff were judged according to their probable effectiveness in bringing about a reduction in the delinquency-prone attitudes of those confined. High-maturity confinees, it was found, performed better upon return to military duty when their therapeutic-community experience had been under effective rather than ineffective supervision. Low-maturity confinees, however, performed much worse upon restoration to duty when they had been under effective supervision than when they had been under supervision judged ineffective.

Recent California studies of parole, group counseling, and vocational training reveal similar interactions. The programs show positive effects for some types of offenders, but no effect or negative effects for other types; the main positive effects took place within the second lowest quartile of the base expectancy distribution. While further replications are needed and are being conducted, present studies strongly suggest that agencies must systematically determine which clients should receive which programs. Further, prediction procedures are proving effective both in providing bases for evaluation and in developing relevant classifications.

PROGRAMS WASTED ON "GOOD RISKS"

To repeat, base expectancy tables can aid in identifying those who will benefit from specific correctional programs. Base expectancies also have identified offenders who will perform with less than the regularly prescribed program. What is more, these "good risk" clients have been found to receive more, than their share of available programing.

California's Department of Corrections experimentally placed good parole risks, as determined by base expectancy rates (best 15 per cent), under minimal supervision. The "good risks" performed as well as they were predicted to do under regular supervision.

The California Women's Parole Division analyzed the frequency of interview contacts for three different base-expectancy-derived classifications and found that the top 15 per cent (good risks) were receiving more than their share of interviews. Partly as a result of these analyses, the Women's Parole Division has developed a new classification and supervisory system. Good risks receive minimal attention. The supervisory time thus saved is redeployed in treatment-oriented supervision of amenable parolees and in surveillance of the nonamenable.

California's Adult Parole Division has developed "good risk" caseloads of male parolees and is using the saved supervisory time for more intensive supervision of "middle risk" parolees—a result of experiments in which a prediction procedure was used to study parole.

SUBJECTIVE DECISIONS ALSO NEED STUDY

In defense of subjectively based as opposed to statistically based decisions, much has been written about the uniqueness of the individual. Kluckholm and Murray, however, suggest that the unique qualities of a client provide only one kind of information which can aid us in making decisions. "Every man is in certain respects (a) like all other men, (b) like some other men, (c) like no other man." All three kinds of information are, and should be, subjected to empirical study.

More needs to be known about human behavior. More needs to be known about prediction devices. Certainly, more needs to be known about predicting future behavior of a person on the basis of past behavior.

The point to emphasize, however, is that to refer to the uniqueness of an individual is to indicate an area of systematic study. It is no justification for making decisions about his future in a sloppy, unsystematic, and costly manner.

As discussed by several, it is not a question of subjective vs.

statistical prediction. Judgments can be used to improve prediction formulas as well as decisions, while statistical study of subjective judgment can improve the judgment.

Perhaps what I have said here can best be summarized by Kelvin's frequently quoted words: "When you can measure what you are speaking about and express it in numbers, you know something about it, but when you cannot measure it, when you cannot express it in numbers your knowledge is of a meagre and unsatisfactory kind."

15

PAROLE ADDENDUM*

IF PRISONERS are to be released at all, they should be released conditionally. It is unimportant what we call this period of adjustment. As parole systems now function, we tend to defeat our purpose. The best risks for successful re-entry into the free community are selected for parole; while the poorest risks for successful adjustment are released without supervision upon the termination of their maximum sentences. Most prisoners could benefit from guidance during the community re-entry process. Most inmates tend to idealize the "outside world" while incarcerated; consequently are in need of a "reality thrust" when they leave the restricted environment of the correctional institution.

The sentencing court performs the rite of "status deprivation" through which the offender looses his civil rights. If the offender is to be returned to the free community, and if he is expected to successfully re-adjust after his incarceration, then what may be needed is a "status restoration" ceremony. When the offender has met the conditions of release, after serving the required part of his sentence, and after a period of non-recidivism (perhaps, 3-5 years), we should provide for a "status restoration" ceremony. This rite should include the automatic expunging of the public record. The stigma of incarceration, the loss of human dignity, deprivation of the right to self determination, plus the discriminatory practices leveled against those with a "record" are not conducive to successful societal participation.

Release procedures must be functionally related to the goal of rehabilitation, if this is the goal of the correctional systems. Thus, all prisoners should be kept under close surveillance immediately following their release, because guidance is critical to the adjustment of the offender as an aid to reorientation, and because supervision should protect society from further redress.

Perhaps, a court approved sponsor who can meet the real needs of the conditionally released prisoner would be a partial solution to

*Barbara A. Kay, Ph.D., and Clyde B. Vedder, Ph.D.

185

the re-entry process of our correctional systems. Now existent parole services could be upgraded if each agent would have fewer parolees to supervise. If the system of court approved sponsors could be extended, parole agents would be used for guidance and supervision only when the authorities deemed the use of skilled professional services advisable.

According to Southerland and Cressey, the condition which probably has the most effect on violation and non-violation of parolees is the behavior of the persons with whom the parolee interacts. We tend to identify with our peers, and we see ourselves through the eyes of our associates. The process through which each person comes to define himself in relation to others of necessity involves social interaction. The offender like all other people sees himself through the eyes of his associates. His definition of himself or self concept is based upon his interpretation of the reactions of other people, to him. Prisonization tends to make the man define himself in terms of an anti-social misfit who has little intrinsic worth. This is why incarceration should be used sparingly, and only when probation and other remedial measures to protect society have failed.

Upon release from prison the offender is in desperate need of a friend, a confidant and resource person. The very act of voluntary sponsorship demonstrates faith in the prisoner's worth which may be the first of many steps in the development of a more positive self concept. Most individuals (including offenders) react to social expectations. The offender defines himself as a person who is expected to violate the law because the reactions to him by important others have led him to this passe. Perhaps, the chief distinction between persons who will and those who will not experience difficulty with the law is to be found in the extent to which a socially acceptable self image has been developed. Incarceration reinforces the offender's criminal self definition. This self concept has its base in learning experiences which are part and parcel of social interaction. Since this negative self definition is arrived at through social interaction it must be resolved through a similar process. The offender can negate his criminal self definition through a guided process of social interaction. It is essential that we provide either a system of sponsorship or a parole system that will guide this social interaction.

A good personal appearance goes a long way in eliciting a positive reaction from those with whom we interact. The facility of regarding oneself as capable or adequate to meet the challenges encountered in life goes a long way in seeing one through structured, as well as unstructured situations. One person (a sponsor or parole agent) who demonstrates his sincere interest and realistic expectations for the offender goes a long way in providing the stimulus for a personal reappraisal. The sponsor or parole agent should be a catalyst to the social interaction process of the offender.

For those offenders who have no community resources, prerelease centers of the type that The Federal Bureau of Prisons is experimenting with should be provided. A half-way-house or center which furnishes the prisoner with a place to live during his readjustment to the free community. Resource persons who are familiar with the problems of ex-convicts are available at all times for help in dealing with crisis situations and long range planning.

Release procedures should be the final step in an integrated system of treatment. Arrest, detention, probation, incarceration and release procedures (parole) should be of comparable quality. All phases of correctional systems should share a philosophy of rehabilitation which must guide their treatment of the offender as they prepare him to live in free community. If prisoners are to be released at all, then the entire correctional process must be geared toward treatment (for the protection of society).

It is estimated that it costs ten times as much to keep an offender in prison as it would cost to provide probation or parole services. (In today's economy it costs approximately $2,000 per year to maintain an offender in prison, while the cost of providing probation or parole services is about $200 per year.) Although cheapness of service is hardly justification for choice of program when the issue is human salvage, the fact remains that offenders can be treated without incarceration several times cheaper than they can when institutionalized. These estimates do not include loss of income while incarcerated, relief to families of prisoners, initial cost of construction, etc.

The antics of the press are reflected in the laymen's opposition to parole. The press tends to dramatically portray violations of parolees, while neglecting parole successes. The public in turn views parole as a form of leniency which is a threat to the public welfare. In fact, parole is not a form of leniency. The parole violator looses credit for time spent outside the prison, should he violate the conditions of parole. This has the effect of extending the period of control by the state over parolees. It is upon this latter basis that many offenders oppose parole.

Authorities should eliminate every unnecessary parole condition that forces men on parole to refrain from what law-abiding citizens do everyday, such as changing jobs, going out of town, buying on credit, or having a glass of beer in their own homes. The only condition of parole which is really necessary is that the parolee behave himself, and assume his responsibilities as a normal, law-abiding citizen. As most parole systems now function, the parolee is expected to be completely normal while entangled in abnormal conditions. Many conditions of parole are unrealistic, impossible to enforce and serve no end. It is true that many stated conditions are not enforced, and if that is the case, how can we expect the parolee to respect the parole agent, the parole system or feel any measure of security within himself, when he knows that enforcement can be (and often is) on the basis of whim.

One of the more hopeless aspects of the correctional process is the ineligibility for parole of many inmates, despite their potential for successful adjustment in the free community. A breakthrough came on September 28, 1962 when the Illinois Supreme Court ruled that "all" prisoners in any of the Illinois Prisons are eligible for parole consideration after serving twenty years. Significantly, this new ruling was made effective immediately and retroactively. As a result over forty inmates at Menard and over 100 inmates at Stateville became eligible for parole consideration. The retroactive feature was decided in a test case in behalf of Stateville inmate, who was sentenced in 1933 to 100 years for robbery and murder of a physician. Under the old Illinois Criminal Code, he would not have been eligible for a parole hearing until he had served one-third of the sentence or about thirty-three years. The appeal was financed by inmates at Stateville, who contributed from $1. to $75. each, since the parole board had interpreted the new ruling to apply only to persons sentenced on or after January 1962. Previous cases had supported the view that there exists a definite relationship between parole eligibility and a sentence. In *People* v. *Pace*, the defendant contended that his sentence of 199 years was illegal because it circumvented the Parole Act; for had he been given a life sentence, he would have been eligible for parole consideration at the end of twenty years, but with a 199 year sentence, having to serve one-third of it would mean he wouldn't live long enough to become eligible for parole. The precedent of the Pace case was followed in *People* v. *Rucker,* that the matter of parole is not a judicial but purely a legislative function," and in *People* v. *Thompson,* that "parole is merely an act of clemency which the defendant cannot invoke at his own will." The "New" interpretation was predicated on the theory that the Illinois Legislature did not indicate it would apply to persons sentenced on or after January 1, 1962, but that *every* person sentenced to the penitentiary regardless of the length of such sentence shall be eligible for parole at the end of twenty years. If the proviso applied only to sentences pronounced on or after January 1, 1962, the application of this proviso would be delayed for twenty years until inmates had served that much of their sentences, hence it would remain ineffective until 1982. Justice House, who wrote the majority opinion stated that it was the *intent* of the legislature to have the parole provision applied retroactively.

But much still remains to be accomplished in the area of parole legislation. Such legislation as was passed in Illinois is a step in the right direction. The parole ideal has not been attained in any state. Although parole is considerably less costly than institutionalized treatment, the press and the public decry large outlays for creating an effective parole service. It is the administration of parole that errs, there is little wrong with parole per se. Parole services could be improved considerably, if the entire correctional process were geared to preparation of prisoners for their inevitable release. Parole is in need of public understanding and support which should be forthcoming as scientific knowledge about human behavior is developed and disseminated.

BIBLIOGRAPHY

Adler, N.: Probation in the Courts. *Journal of Comparative Legislation and International Law, 17:* (1935) pp. 286–288.

Affleck, D. M.: Therapeutic Utilization of Probation Authority Vested in a Private Agency. *Journal of Social Work Process, 1:* (1937) pp. 104–126.

Allen, R. M.: Problems of Parole, *Journal of Criminal Law, Criminology, and Police Science, 38:* (1947–48) pp. 7–13.

American Correctional Association: *A Manual of Correctional Standards* (1959).

American Prison Association: *Handbook on Pre-release Preparation in Correctional Institutions* (1948).

Arluke, N. R.: A Summary of Parole Rules. *Journal of the National Probation and Parole Association.* (January 1956). pp. 6–13.

Austin, Lucille Nickel: Some Notes about Case Work in Probation Agencies. *Family, 18:* (1937) pp. 282–285.

Australian Council of Education Research: *Probation for Juvenile Delinquents.* Melbourne, Australian Council of Educational Research, 1941.

Barnes, Harry Elmer, and Negley K. Teeters: *New Horizons in Criminology,* 3rd Edition. Englewood Cliffs, N. J., Prentice-Hall, Inc., 1959.

Bartoo, Chester H.: Interviewing Candidates for Probation. *Federal Probation, 25:* (March 1961) pp. 19–28.

Bassin, Alexander: Effect of Group Therapy Upon Certain Attitudes and Perceptions of Adult Offenders on Probation. Unpublished Ph.D. dissertation, New York University.

Bates, Sanford: *Prisons and Beyond.* New York, Macmillian, 1936.

——: Probation and Parole as Elements in Crime Prevention. *Law and Contemporary Problems, 1:* (1934) pp. 484–493.

——: The Establishment and Early Years of the Federal Probation System. *Federal Probation, 14:* (1950) No. 2, pp. 16–21.

Bean, W. J.: How a Federal Institution Prepares its Prisoners for Return to Society. *Federal Probation* (December 1953) pp. 34–38.

Beard, Belle Boone: Juvenile Probation: *An Analysis of the Case Records of Five Hundred Children Studied at the Judge Baker Guidance Clinic and Placed on Probation in the Juvenile Court of Boston.* New York, American Book Co., 1934.

Bell, M., and C. L. Chute: *Crime, Courts, and Probation.* New York, Macmillan, 1956.

Bennett, James V.: The Co-ordination of Probation, Parole and Institutional Treatment. *National Probation Association Yearbook* (1937) pp. 122–129.

Benton, F. M.: Supervising the Adult Parolee. *Journal of the National Probation and Parole Association* (1948) pp. 202–210.

Betts, Isabel: Six Months Experience with a Parolee Classification System. *The Research Newsletter,* No. 3–4 (Sept.–Dec. 1961) .

Bixby, F. Lovell, and Lloyd W. McCorkle: Applying the Principles of Group Therapy in Correctional Institutions. *Federal Probation* (March 1950) pp. 36–40.

Blake, Marilyn A.: Probation Is Not Casework. *Federal Probation, 12:* (1948) No. 2, pp. 54–57.

Blanshard, Paul, and Edwin J. Lukas: *Probation and Psychiatric Care for Adolescent Offenders in New York City.* New York, Society for the Prevention of Crime, 1942.

Breckinridge, Sophonisba P.: *Social Work and the Courts.* Chicago, Univ. of Chicago Press, 1934.

Brewer: The Clerk Also Has an Important Part in Probation. *Federal Probation* (July 1955) pp. 6–9.

Bridges, F.: The Personal Interview. *Journal of the National Probation and Parole Association* (1953) pp. 34–37.

Brill, Jeanette G., and Enoch G. Payne: *Adolescent Court and Crime Prevention.* New York, Pitman, 1938.

Bronner, Augusta F.: Techniques in Interviewing. *Federal Probation, 7:* (1943) No. 3, pp. 10–13.

Brown, L. Guy: A Working Philosophy for the Probation and Parole Officer. *Federal Probation, 7:* (1943) , No. 4, pp. 19–23.

Bruce, Andrew A., Albert J. Harno, John Landesco, and Ernest W. Burgess: *The Working of the Indeterminate Sentence Law and the Parole System in Illinois.* Springfield, Parole Board, 1928.

Burbank, E. G.: The Place of Social Casework Service in the Pre-release Program of the Correctional Institution. *Proceedings of the American Prison Association* (1948) pp. 252–260.

——, and E. W. Goldsborough: The Probation Officer's Personality: A Key Factor in Rehabilitation. *Federal Probation* (June 1954) pp. 11–14.

Campbell, Judge William J.: Developing Systematic Sentencing Procedures. *Federal Probation* (September 1954) .

Cantor, Nathaniel F.: *Crime, Criminals and Criminal Justice.* New York, Henry Holt, 1932.

——: *Crime and Society: An Introduction to Criminology.* New York, Henry Holt, 1939.

——: The Function of Probation. in *National Probation Association, Yearbook* (1941) pp. 277–297.

Carroll, Helen M., and Frank J. Curran: A Follow-up Study of Three-Hundred Court Cases from the Adolescent Ward of Bellevue Hospital. *Mental Hygiene, 24:* (1940) , pp. 621–638.

Chandler, Henry P.: Probation: What It Can Do and What It Takes. *Federal Probation* (March 1948) pp. 11–16.

——: The Future of Federal Probation. *Federal Probation, 14:* (1950) No. 2, pp. 41–48.

Chappell, Richard A.: *Decisions Interpreting the Federal Probation Act.* Washington, D.C., U.S. Bureau of Prisons, 1937.

——: Developing Workers on the Job. *National Probation Association, Yearbook,* 1942, pp. 276–281.

——: The Federal Probation Service: Its Growth and Progress. *Federal Probation, 11:* (1947) No. 4. pp. 29–34.

——: The Federal Probation System Today. *Federal Probation, 14:* (1950), No. 2, pp. 30–40.

Cherry, Ethel N.: Supervision of Workers in a Probation Department, with discussion by Randel Shake. *National Probation Association, Yearbook* (1940) pp. 254–270.

——: The Probation Officer on the Job. *National Probation Association, Yearbook* (1945) pp. 195–206.

Chute, Charles Lionel: State Supervision of Probation Work. *Journal of Criminal Law and Criminology, 8:* (1918) pp. 923–928.

——: The Development and Needs of Probation Service. *Journal of Criminal Law and Criminology, 18:* (1928) pp. 514–521.

——: The Extension of Probation in Criminal Courts. *American Academy of Political and Social Science, 136:* (1928) pp. 136–141.

——: State Participation in Probation Work. In *National Probation Association, Yearbook* (1931) pp. 169–179.

——: The Progress of Probation and Social Treatment in Courts. *Journal of Criminal Law and Criminology, 24:* (1933) pp. 60–73.

——: Developing Successful Probation Personnel. *Proceedings of the American Prison Association, 66:* (1936) pp. 86–94.

——: Probation versus Jail. *Jail Association Journal* (January 1940).

——: The Development and Expansion of Probation. *Proceedings of the American Prison Association* (1945) pp. 90–93.

——: The Campaign for Federal Probation. *Federal Probation, 14:* (1950), No. 2, pp. 3–9.

——, and M. Bell: *Crime, Courts and Probation.* New York, Macmillan, 1956.

Clark, R. E.: Size of the Parole Community as Related to Parole Outcome. *American Journal of Sociology, 57:* (1951) pp. 43–47.

Class, N. E.: Qualifications: A Realistic Approach to Personnel Requirements. *Journal of the National Probation and Parole Association* (April 1957) pp. 107–110.

Clemmer, Donald: *The Prison Community.* New York, Rinehart, 1940.

Clinard, Marshall B.: Prediction of Recidivism. In *Review of Sociology.* New York, John Wiley and Sons, 1957, pp. 485–488.

Clink, Stephen H., and Millard Prichard: Casework in a Juvenile Court. *Family, 25:* (1944) pp. 304–309.

Committee for the Study of Probation Services: *Probation Services in California 1948–1949* (1949).

Coddington, F.J.O.: The Probation System Under the Criminal Justice Act.

In L. Radzinowicz, and J.W.C. Turner (eds.) *The Journal of Criminal Science,* Vol. 2 (1950) , pp. 23–45.

Cohen, Irving E.: Probation as a Social Casework Process. *National Probation Association, Yearbook* (1945) , pp. 207–216.

Colcord, Joanna C.: Probation Officer as a Social Worker. *Probation* New York, 9: (Nov. 1930) pp. 1–2, 6.

Cooley, Edwin J.: *New Goals in Probation.* Albany, N.Y., New York State Probation Commission, 1926.

——: *Probation and Delinquency: The Study and Treatment of the Individual Delinquent.* New York, Catholic Charities, 1927.

Cooper, H. Homfray (ed.) : *Probation.* London, Shaw and Sons Ltd., 1949.

Cosulich, Gilbert: *Adult Probation Laws of the United States.* New York, National Probation Association, 1940.

——: Probation and Parole Publicity in the Press. *National Probation Association, Yearbook* (1940) pp. 271–281.

Cozart, Reed: Release Preparation of the Offender. *Federal Probation* (March 1952) pp. 13–16.

Crihfield, B. E.: The Interstate Parole and Probation Compact. *Federal Probation* (June 1953) pp. 3–7.

Crystal, David: Family Casework in Probation. *Federal Probation, 13:* (1949) No. 4, pp. 47–53.

Cunningham, E. B.: The Role of the Parole Advisor, *Federal Probation* (December 1951) pp. 43–46.

Dalton, R. H.: Value and Use of Counseling Techniques in the Work of Probation Officers. *Federal Probation* (December 1952) .

Davis, M. P.: Further Implementation of the Interstate Parole Compact. *Proceedings of American Prison Association* (1949) pp. 259–262.

Dayton, Joseph E.: The Part that Prisoners' Aid Associations Have Played in the Advancement of Probation, Parole and Prison Management. *Proceedings of American Prison Association* (1934) pp. 327–335.

Dempsey, D. and D. Herr: His Best Friends are Convicts. *Coronet* (June 1949) .

Deutschberger, Paul: Case Work Failures and the Psychology of Restriction. *Probation* (New York, 1946) pp. 103–108.

Dobbs, Harrison A.: Social Service for Probationers and Parolees. *Focus, 28:* (1949) pp. 7–12.

Doyle, R. F.: Conditions of Probation. *Federal Probation* (Sept. 1953) pp. 19–22.

Dressler, David: Case Work with the Adult Offender. *National Probation Association Yearbook* (1942) pp. 177–188.

——: *Probation and Parole.* Columbia University Press, 1951.

——: *Parole Chief.* Viking Press, 1951.

Duffy, F. Ryan: Value of the Presentence Investigation Reports to the Court. *Federal Probation, 5:* (1941) No. 3, pp. 3–5.

Edson, L.: Tales of a Parole Board Chief. *Saturday Evening Post* (June 30, 1951.

Eliot, Thomas D.: Case Work Functions and Judicial Functions: Their Co-ordination. *National Probation Association Yearbook* (1937) pp. 252–266.

Elkin, Winifred A.: *English Juvenile Courts.* London, Kegan Paul, Trench, Trubner & Co., 1938.

Ellis, William J.: Interstate Parole and Probation Compact: An Appraisal After Ten Years of Operation. *State Government, 18:* (1945) pp. 40–42.

England, Ralph W., Jr.: Some Dangers in Parole Prediction. *National Council on Crime and Delinquency Journal 8:* (July 1962) pp. 265–269.

Evjen, Victor H.: Current Thinking of Parole Prediction Tables. *National Council on Crime and Delinquency Journal, 8:* (July 1962) pp. 215–238.

Farrow, R. G.: The Give and Take of Parole Supervision. *Focus* (Jan. 1953) pp. 1–5.

——, and G. I. Giardini: The Paroling of Capital Offenders. *Annals* (Nov. 1952) pp. 85–94.

Fenton, N.: The Psychological Preparation of Inmates for Release. *Proceedings of American Prison Association* (1949) pp. 100–110.

Ferris, Ralph H.: Integrating Probation Service on a Statewide Basis. *National Probation Association, Yearbook* (1939) pp. 218–231.

Fink, Arthur E.: Probation Officers Broaden Their Horizons. *Federal Probation, 4:* (1940) No. 3 pp. 32–33.

——: Parole Supervision — A Case Analysis. *Federal Probation* (Sept. 1951) pp. 39–45.

Finsley, F.: Who Gets Parole. *Federal Probation* (Sept. 1953) pp. 26–29.

Fishman, J. F., and V. Perlman: In the Name of Parole. *Yale Review, 28:* (1939).

——: A Critical Review of Probation and Parole. *National Probation and Parole Association, Yearbook* (1953) pp. 3–23.

Fitzgerald, E.: The Presentence Investigation. *Journal of the National Probation and Parole Association* (Oct. 1956) pp. 320–326.

Flexner, Bernard, and Roger N. Baldwin: *Juvenile Courts and Probation.* New York, Century Co., 1916.

Floch, M.: Mental Hygiene in Parole Work. *Focus* (January 1955) pp. 15–17.

Flynn, Frank T.: Training for the Probation Profession. *Federal Probation, 4:* (1940) No. 1, pp. 11–14.

——: Probation and Individualized Justice. *Federal Probation, 14:* (1950) No. 2, pp. 70–76.

——: Parole Supervision — a Case Analysis. *Federal Probation* (June 1951) pp. 36–42.

Fry, Margery, Max Grünhut, Herman Mannheim, Wanda Grabinska, C. D. Rackham, *et al.: A Policy for the Juvenile Courts Prepared by the International Committee of the Howard League for Penal Reform, 1942–1945.* London, Allen & Unwin, 1947.

Fuller, J. K.: Extension of Group Therapy to Parolees. *Prison World* (July-Aug. 1952) pp. 8–11.

Galvin, John J.: Progressive Developments in Pre-release Preparation. *Proceedings of American Prison Association* (1948) pp. 243–251.

——: Planning a Pre-Release Unit Program. *Proceedings of American Prison Association* (1950) pp. 144–149.

——: Evaluating the Work of Parole Officers. *National Probation and Parole Association, Yearbook* (1953) pp. 38–42.

Giardini, G. I.: *The Parole Process.* Charles C Thomas, Publisher, Springfield, Illinois, 1959.

Gillin, John L.: Parole Prediction in Wisconsin. *Sociology and Social Research, 34:* (1950) pp .407–414.

——, and Reuben L. Hill: Success and Failure of Adults Probationers in Wisconsin. *Journal of Criminal Law and Criminology, 30:* (1940) pp. 807–829.

Glaser, Daniel: A Reconsideration of Some Parole Prediction Factors. *American Sociological Review* (June 1954) pp. 335–341.

——: Testing Correctional Decisions *Journal of Criminal Law, Criminology and Police Science* (Mar.-Apr. 1955) pp. 679–684.

——: The Efficacy of Alternative Approaches to Parole Prediction. *American Sociological Review* (June 1955) pp. 283–287.

Glover, Elizabeth R.: *Probation and Re-education.* London, Routledge & Kegan Paul Ltd., 1949.

Glueck, Sheldon (ed.) : *Probation and Criminal Justice.* New York, Macmillan, 1933.

——, and Eleanor T. Glueck: *500 Criminal Careers.* New York, Alfred A. Knopf, 1930.

——: *One Thousand Juvenile Delinquents.* Cambridge, Mass., Harvard Univ. Press, 1934.

Goldsborough, E. W., and E. G. Burbank: The Probation Offcer's Personality: a Key factor in Rehabilitation. *Federal Probation* (June 1954) pp. 11–14.

Gondree, H.: Institutional Training Should Prepare for Parole. *Federal Probation* (Sept. 1951) pp. 31-34.

Goodman, L. A.: The Use and Validity of a Prediction Instrument. *American Sociological Review, 58:* (1953) pp. 503–512.

Gordon, W. A.: California Adult Authority. *Proceedings of American Prison Association* (1947) pp. 215–220.

——: An Experiment in Intensive Supervision. *Focus* (Mar. 1954) pp. 33–36.

Gottshall, A. E.: Leading Court Decisions Affecting Federal Probation. *Federal Probation, 14:* (1950) No. 2, pp. 76–83.

Graham, M. R.: *These Came Back.* (Univ. of Alabama, Bur. Pub. Adm. 1946) .

Grant, J. Douglas: It's Time to Start Counting. *National Council on Crime and Delinquency 8:* (July 1962) pp. 259–264.

Grinnell, Frank W.: Probation as an Orthodox Common Law Practice in

Massachusetts Prior to the Statutory System. *Massachusetts Law Quarterly,* *2:* (1916-17) pp. 591–639.

——: The Common Law History of Probation: An Illustration of the 'Equitable' Growth of Criminal Law. *Journal of Criminal Law and Criminology, 32:* (1941) pp. 15–34.

Grünhut, Max: *Penal Reform, A Comparitive Study,* See, in particular, Ch. XII, Non-Institutional Treatment. Oxford Univ. Press, 1948.

Gurham, I.: Community Discrimination Against the Parolee, *Focus* (Nov. 1953) pp. 163–168.

Hakeem, Michael: Glueck Method of Parole Prediction Applied to 1,861 Cases of Burglars. *Journal of Criminal Law and Criminology, 36:* (1945–46) pp. 87–97.

——: The Validity of the Burgess Method of Parole Prediction. *American Sociological Review, 53:* (1948) pp. 376–386.

——: Prediction of Parole Outcome from Summaries of Case Histories. *Journal of Criminal Law, Criminology and Police Science* (July-August 1961) pp. 145–155.

Hall, Gladys E.: Social Case Work in Probation and Parole. *National Probation Association, Yearbook* (1942) pp. 121–132.

Halpern, Irving W.: Practical Problems in Administering Probation. *National Probation Association, Yearbook* (1931) pp. 105–119.

——: A Decade of Probation. New York, Court of General Sessions: 1938.

——: Interpretation of Probation to the Public. *Proceedings of American Prison Association* (1939) pp. 106–112.

——: Probation Treatment is Planned. *Federal Probation* (Jan. 1947) pp. 38–41.

Hannum, R. R.: Employment Problems of Ex-Offender. *Focus* (Nov. 1954) pp. 184–187.

Harper, William J.: Practical Training for Probation Work. *Proceedings American Prison Association* (1937) pp. 130–134.

Harris, J.: Probation: *Thirty-four Years' Work in Local Police Courts.* London, Lowestoft, 1937.

Harris, Seymour F.: *Principles and Practice of the Criminal Law.* 17th ed. Rewritten and enlarged by A. M. Wilshire. London, Sweet & Maxwell, 1943.

Harris, S. W.: *Probation and Other Social Work of the Courts,* London, Clarke Hall Fellowship, 1937.

——: New Concepts in Release Procedures. *Proceedings of American Prison Association* (1953) pp. 245–249.

Harrison, Gus: The Michigan Parole Camp. *Focus* (March 1954) pp. 37–42.

Hart, Hornell: Predicting Parole Success. *Journal of Criminal Law and Criminology* (November 1923).

Hartwell, Samuel W.: Personality of the Probation Officer. *Federal Probation, 10:* (1946) No. 1, pp. 27–31.

Haskell, Samuel B.: Classification in the Treatment of Adult Probationers. *National Probation Association, Yearbook* (1937) pp. 161–175.

Harvard Law Review Assn.: Parole Revocation Procedures. *Harvard Law Review, 65:* (1951) pp. 309–315.

Havel, Joan, and Elaine Sulka: Special Intensive Parole Unit, Phase III. *Research Report No. 3,* California Dept. of Corrections (March 1962).

Hayner, Norman S.: Summary of Discussion on Parole Hearings, Policy, Etc. *Proceedings of American Prison Association* (1952) pp. 326–328.

——: Sentencing by an Administrative Board. *Law and Contemporary Social Problems, Duke Univ. School of Law* (Summer 1958).

——: Why Do Parole Boards Lag in the Use of Prediction Scores. *The Pacific Sociological Review.* Vol. 1, No. 2 (Fall 1958) pp. 73–76.

Head, W. J.: Job Finding for Prisoners. *Federal Probation* (March 1952) pp. 20–25.

Healy, William, and Augusta Bronner: *Delinquents and Criminals: Their Making and Unmaking.* New York, Macmillan, 1926.

——: New Light on Delinquency and Its Treatment. New Haven, Yale Univ. Press, 1936.

Hendrick, E. J.: Conditions and Violations of Probation and Parole. *National Probation and Parole Association, Yearbook* (1951) pp. 41–48.

——: Basic Concepts of Conditions and Violations. *Journal of the National Probation and Parole Association* (Jan. 1956) pp. 1–5.

Hill, Matthew Davenport: *Suggestions for the Repression of Crime Contained in Charges Delivered to Grand Juries of Birmingham: Supported by Additional Facts and Arguments* (London, 1857).

Hiller, F.: Adult Probation in the United States. *National Probation and Parole Association, Yearbook* (1933).

——: Methods of Appointing Probation Officers. *Journal of the National Probation and Parole Association* (April 1957) pp. 120–128.

Hoey, Jane M.: The Place of Probation Service in the Social Work of a Community. *Proceedings of New York State Conference of Probation Officers, 21:* (1928) pp. 194–198.

Hoffman, L. Wallace: Developing Attitudes through Supervision. *National Probation and Parole Association, Yearbook* (1939) pp. 98–115.

——: Guidance Clinic: Its Place in the Probation Officer's Program. *Federal Probation, 6:* (1942), No. 2, pp. 9–13.

Holton, Karl: A Yardstick for Measuring Probation. *Federal Probation, 7:* (1943) No, 1, pp. 41–43.

Homer, Paul: Tying the Clinic with the Court. *National Probation and Parole Association, Yearbook* (1941) pp. 167–180.

Hoover, J. Edgar: Dangerous Freedom. *American Magazine* (January 1948).

Hughes, E. P.: *The Probation System in America.* London, Howard Assn., 1903.

Hughes, E. W.: An Analysis of the Records of Some 750 Probationers. *British Journal of Educational Psychology, 13:* (1943) pp. 113–125.

Hyman, E. C.: Holding the Promiscuous Girl Accountable for Her Own Behavior. *National Probation and Parole Association Journal* (1948) pp. 189–201.

Huffman, A. V. and W. M. Meeks: A statement of Principles of Treatment in Preparation for Parole. *Federal Probation* (Dec. 1954) pp. 9–14.

Illinois Dept. of Public Safety: *Rules and Statutes Governing Restoration of Citizenship Rights to Discharged Probationers and Discharged Prisoners* (1949).

Illinois Law Review: The Parole System in Illinois, *45:* (1950) pp. 407–414.

Jacks, W. L.: *A Comparison of Parole Agents' Salaries, Caseloads, and Supervision Duties.* Pennsylvania Board of Parole, 1957.

Jaffary, Stuart K.: Probation for the Adult Offender. In symposium on Penal Reform in Canada. *Canadian Bar Review, 27:* (1949) pp. 1020–1040.

Jenkins, R. L., Henry Harper Hart, Philip I. Sperling, and Sidney Axelrad: Prediction of Parole Success. Inclusion of Psychiatric Criteria. *Journal of Criminal Law and Criminology* (May 1942).

Johnson, Fred R.: *Probation of Juveniles and Adults: A Study of Principles and Methods.* New York, Century Co., 1928.

Kawin, Irene: Legal Handicaps in Juvenile Case Work. *National Probation and Parole Association* (1937) pp. 188–202.

Keve, Paul: *Prison, Probation, or Parole.* Univ. of Minn. Press, 1954.

——: *The Probation Officer Investigates.* Univ. of Minn. Press, 1961.

Killinger, G.: The Federal Government's Parole Program. *Federal Probation* (June 1950) pp. 56–64.

——: The Functions and Responsibilities of Parole Boards. *National Probation and Parole Association* (1950) pp. 121–129.

Kirby, B. C.: Parole Prediction Using Multiple Correlation. *American Journal of Sociology* (May 1954) pp. 539–550.

Kirkpatrick, A. M.: After-Care in the Canadian Correctional Treatment Plan. *ACA* (1953) pp. 225–232.

League of Nations. Advisory Committee on Social Questions: *Principles Applicable to the Functioning of Juvenile Courts and Similar Bodies.* Auxiliary Services and Institutions, Geneva, League of Nations, 1937.

——: Child Welfare Committee (in collaboration with the International Prison Commission): *Organization of Juvenile Courts and Results Attained Hitherto.* Geneva, League of Nations, 1931).

——: Child Welfare Committee: *Auxiliary Services of Juvenile Courts.* Geneva, League of Nations, 1931).

——: Child Welfare Committee (in collaboration with the International Penal and Penitentiary Commission): *Organization of Juvenile Courts and Results Attained Hitherto.* Geneva, League of Nations, 1935.

——: Child Welfare Committee: *Child Welfare Councils.* Denmark, Norway, Sweden. Geneva, League of Nations, 1937.

Lejins, Peter P.: Criminology for Probation and Parole Officers. *Journal of the National Probation and Parole Association* (July, 1956), pp. 200–207.

——: Parole Prediction an Introductory Statement. *National Council on Crime and Delinquency Journal, 8:* (July, 1962), pp. 209–214.

Le Mesurier, L. (ed.) : *A Handbook of Probation and Social Work of the Courts.* London, National Association of Probation Officers, 1935; Supplement, 1943.

Lenroot, Katharine F., and Emma O. Lundberg: *Juvenile Courts at Work: A Study of the Organization and Methods of Ten Courts.* Washington, Government Printing Office, 1925.

Lester, Ervis: Parole Treatment and Surveillance—Which Should Dominate? *American Prison Association* (1952) pp. 46–60.

Lippman, H. S.: The Role of the Probation Officer in the Treatment of Delinquency in Children. *Federal Probation* (June, 1948) pp. 36–39.

——: Pre-release Preparation of Parolees. *Focus* (Sept. 1952) pp. 135–139.

Long, H. S.: *The First Hundred Days.* National Probation and Parole Association (1953) pp. 31–33.

Long, Jean: Problems of Job Placement for Overtime Inmates. *American Prison Association* (1952) pp. 61–70.

Loos, A. R.: Telling the Community about the Offender. *Correction,* New York (July, 1952).

Lou, Herbert H.: *Juvenile Courts in the United States.* Chapel Hill, N. C., Univ. of North Carolina Press, 1927.

Loveland, F.: Financial and Material Aspects of Release Planning. *Federal Probation* (March 1952) pp. 17–20.

Lowry, Fern: *Readings in Social Case Work, 1920–1938:* Selected Readings for the Case Work Practitioner. New York, Columbia Univ. Press, 1939.

Lykke, Arthur F.: Parade and Payrolls, Springfield, Illinois, Charles C Thomas, Publisher, 1957.

Maeder, LeRoy M. A.: Generic Aspects of the Intake Interview. *Family, 23:* (1942) pp. 14–23.

Mannheim, H. and L. T. Wilkins: *Prediction Methods in Relation to Borstal Training.* London, Her Majesty's Stationery Office, 1955.

Martin, J. B.: The Case of Anne Martin — Ex-Convict. *Saturday Evening Post* (July 7, 1951).

Master, J. M.: The Relation of Judicial Selection to Successful Probation *Federal Probation 12:* (1948) No. 1, pp. 36–41.

——: Legislative Background of the Federal Probation Act. *Federal Probation., 14:* (1950) No. 2, pp. 9–16.

Massachusetts, Commission on Probation. *Reports on an Inquiry into the Permanent Results of Probation.* Massachusetts Senate Document No. 431, 1924.

McDivitt, C. B.: Reintegration of the Offender in the Community. *Proceedings of American Prison Association,* (1949), pp. 126–131.

McGrath, William A.: Case Work in an Authoritarian Setting. *National Probation Association Yearbook,* (1937), pp. 176–187.

McHugh, T. J.: Requirements for Parole Selection. *Proceedings of American Prison Association,* (1949) , pp. 170–174.

——: Practical Aspects of Casework in Parole Supervision. *National Probation and Parole Association,* (1950) , pp. 158–169.

——: Parole from Within the Institution. *Focus,* (January, 1948) , pp. 13–18.

McMinn, E.: The Institutional Parole Officer. *Focus* (January, 1954) , pp. 21–24.

McRuer. J. C.: Sentences. In symposium on Penal Reform in Canada. *Canadian Bar Review, 27:* (1949) pp. 1001–1019.

Meachem, William S.: Conditions of Probation and Parole——Do They Help or Hinder? *National Probation and Parole Association, Yearbook* (1947) , pp. 50–59.

——: Probation and Parole in the Public View. *National Probation and Parole Association* (1946) , pp. 218–223.

Mead, B.: Evaluating the Results of Probation. *Journal of Criminal Law and Criminology 23:* (1932) pp. 631–638.

Meeker, Ben: Probation is Casework? *Federal Probation 12:* (1948) , pp. 51–54.

——: The Federal Probation Service Training Center. *Federal Probation,* (December, 1951) , pp. 31–36.

Meyer, Adolf: Thirty-five Years of Psychiatry in the United States and Our Present Outlook, *American Journal of Psychiatry* (July, 1928)

Meyer, Charles H. Z.: Inservice Training Programs. *National Probation and Parole Association Yearbook* (1942) pp. 263–275.

——: A Half Century of Probation and Parole. *Journal of Criminal Law, Criminology and Police Science, 42:* (1952) pp. 707–728.

Mill, James: *Probation, an Instrument of Imaginative Justice.* London, Clarke Hall Fellowship, 1946.

Miller, F. P.: Parole and the Aftercare Agency. *Canadian Welfare,* (December, 1956) pp. 313–317.

Miller, Justin: The Place of Probation in the Criminal Court. *National Probation and Parole Association Yearbook,* (1939) , pp. 243–265.

Minn, William G.: Training for the Work of a Probation Officer in England and Wales. in L. Radzinoqicz and J.W.C. Turner (eds) , *The Journal of Criminal Science,* Vol. 1 (1948) , pp. 165–172.

——: Probation Work, in Cherry Morris (ed) , *Social Case-Work,* London: Faber Ltd., 1950, pp. 127–142.

Mitchell, E.: Probation Work in Canada. *Fortnightly Law Journal,* Vol. 17, (1948) , pp. 248–250.

Monachesi Elio David: Prediction Factors in Probation: A Study of 1515 Probation Cases of Ramsey County, Minn., 1923-1925, Hanover, N. H. Sociological Press, 1932.

——: American Studies in the Prediction of Recidivism, *Journal of Criminal Law and Criminology,* Vol. 41, (1950-1951) , pp. 268–289.

Moore, Joel R.: The United States Probation System, *Journal of Criminal Law and Criminology,* Vol. 23, (1932), pp. 638–648.

Moreland, Donald W.: John Augustus and His Successors, *National Probation and Parole Association Yearbook,* (1941), pp. 1–23.

Morrison, A. C. K., and Edward Hughes: *The Criminal Justice Act,* (1948) London, Butterwork. 1949 *Annotated.*

Murphy, J. P. and J. Rumney: *Probation and Social Adjustment,* Rutgers University Press, 1952.

Murphy, Joseph P.: A Case Study to Test the Efficiency of Probation Treatment, *Catholic Charities Review,* Vol. 5, (1921), pp. 287–293.

——: Probationer and the Probation Officer, *Federal Probation,* Vol, 10, (1946), pp. 32–35.

Murrah, Alfred: Prison or Probation—Which and Why? *Journal Criminal Law and Criminology,* Vol. 47, (Nov.-Dec., 1956), pp. 451–456.

National Probation and Parole Association, *A Standard Juvenile Court Act,* 1949, Rev. Ed New York: 1949.

National Probation and Parole Association, *The Standard Probation and Parole Act,* 1955.

National Probation Association, *Standards for Selection of Probation and Parole Officers,* New York, 1945.

——, *John Augustus: First Probation Officer.* New York: National Probation Association, 1939.

Newman, Charles L.: *Sourcebook on Probation, Parole and Pardons,* Springfield, Illinois: Charles C Thomas, Publisher, 1958.

New York, State of, Commission to Investigate Prison Administration and Construction, *Probation in New York State,* Albany, N. Y.: J. B. Lyon, 1933.

——Dept. of Correction, Division of Probation, *Manual for Probation Officers in New York State,* 5th ed., Albany, N. Y. State Dept. of Correction, Division of Probation, 1945.

——Division of Parole, *Parole Officers Manual.*

——An Approach to the Study of Delinquencies among Parolees, *Correction,* New York (Nov, 1953), pp. 12–14.

New York Prison Association: Ten Years Experience in a Scientific Approach to the Evaluation of Parole, *Annual Report,* 1949.

Nutt, Alice Scott: The Future of the Juvenile Court as a Case Work Agency, *National Probation and Parole Association Yearbook,* (1939), pp. 157–170.

——Juvenile and Domestic Relations Courts, *Social Work Year Book,* New York: Russell Sage Foundation, 1947. pp. 271–277.

Odell, C. E.: Job Adjustment for Probationers and Parolees, *Federal Probation,* (June, 1951) pp. 12–15.

Ohlin, Lloyd E.: *Selection for Parole,* New York: Russell Sage Foundation 1951.

——, and Otis Dudley Duncan: The Efficiency of Prediction in Criminology, *The American Journal of Sociology*, (March, 1949).

——The Routinization of Correctional Change, *Journal of Criminal Law and Criminology*, Vol. 45: (1954), pp. 400–411.

——*Sociology and the Field of Corrections*, Russell Sage Foundation, 1956.

Oswald, R. D.: Community Discrimination against the Parolee——a second look, *Focus*, (May, 1954), pp. 84–85.

Page, Leo: "Probation as a Treatment of Crime," *Nineteenth Century*, Vol. 120, (1936), pp. 216–226.

——*The Probation System, A Memorandum for Justices*, London: The Clarke Hall Fellowship, n.d.

Paine, E. Clemence: Probation, *Howard Journal*, Vol. 4, (1935), pp. 168–173.

Palmer, Leo J.: *Psychiatry and Social Adjustment of Probationers*, Albany: N. Y.: N. Y. State Dept. of Correction, Division of Probation, 1932.

Patterson, W. K.: A New Parole System, *Focus*, (July, 1954), pp. 121–126.

Perlman, V. and Fishman, J. F.: In the Name of Parole, *Yale Review*, Vol. 28, (1939).

Pigeon, Helen D.: *Probation and Parole in Theory and Practice. A Study Manual*, New York: National Probation Association, 1942.

——et al: *Principles and Methods in Dealing with Offenders*. State College, Pa: Pennsylvania Municipal Publications Service, 1941.

——In-Service Training for Probation and Parole Officers, *Federal Probation*, Vol. 5, (1941), pp. 8–14.

Plummer, E. C.: An Honor Cottage Experiment, *American Prison Association:* Vol. 124, 1950.

Podair, S. and B. I., Tabb: Group Education with Parolees, *Federal Probation*, (Sept, 1954), pp. 33–37.

Prigmore, S. S.: Surveillance or Treatment—the Supervisor's Decision, *Focus*, (January, 1955), pp. 8–11.

——The Role of the Supervisor in Acvhieving a Balance between surveillance and Treatment in Probation and Parole, *American Prison Association*. (1954), pp. 175–180.

Pray, Kenneth L. M.: Place of Social Case Work in the Treatment of Delinquency, *Social Service Review*, Chicago, Vol. 19, (1945) pp. 235–244.

——The Principles of Social Case Work as applied to Probation and Parole, *Federal Probation*, Vol. 9, (1945), pp. 14–18.

Rackham, C. D.: The Probation System, in L. Radzinowicz and J. W. C. Turner (eds.) *Penal Reform in England*, 2nd ed, London: Macmillan, 1946, pp. 118–127.

Radzinowicz, Leon: The After-conduct of Discharged Offenders, in L. Radzinowicz and J. W. C. Turner (eds.) *The Modern Approach to Criminal Law*, London: Macmillan, 1945, pp. 142–161.

——and J. W. C. Turner (eds.), *Conviction and Probation*. (Reprint from *Canadian Bar Review*, September, 1941).

Rappaport, Mazie F.: The Possibility of Help for the Prostitute through Functional Case Work in an Authoritative Setting, In Rosa Wessel (ed) *A Case Work Approach to Sex Delinquency,* Philadelphia: Pennsylvania School of Social Work, 1947.

Ray, J. M.: Scientific Parole—a Proposal, *Journal of Criminal Law and Criminology,* Vol. 37, (1946–1947), pp. 384–389.

——Training Probation and Parole Personnel, *Focus,* Vol. 27, (1948), pp. 44–48.

Reckless, W. C.: Significant Trends in the Treatment of Crime and Delinquency, *Federal Probation,* (March, 1949), pp. 6–11.

Reeves, Wilmer W.: Case Work with the Adult Probationer, *National Probation and Parole Association Yearbook,* (1936), pp. 222–232.

. . . .A Fresh Look at Prediction and Supervision, *National Council on Crime and Delinquency* (January, 1961). pp. 37–41.

Reinemann, John Otto: Developing Community Understanding of Probation and Parole Work, *Journal of Criminal Law and Criminology,* Vol. 33, (1942), pp. 23–31.

——Research Activities in the Probation Department, *National Probation and Parole Association Yearbook* (1946), pp. 196–217.

——Principles and Practices of Probation, *Federal Probation,* September, (1950).

——*Parole and Probation,* Philadelphia Junior Chamber of Commerce, 1955.

Resko, J.: *Reprieve,* Doubleday and Company, 1956.

Richardson, S.: Parole and the Law, National Probation and Parole Association Journal, (Jan, 1956), pp. 27–32.

Rikelman, H. and M. H. Weiss: A Cooperative Effort in Finding Jobs for Prisoners, *Correction,* New York, (June, 1953), pp. 19–22.

Robison, Sophia M.: Chap. 16, Juvenile Probation, *Juvenile Delinquency* New York: Holt, Rinehart and Winston, Inc., 1960, pp. 269–290.

Robinson, Virginia P.: *Supervision in Social Case Work: A Problem in Professional Education,* Chapel Hill, N. C.: Univ. North Carolina Press, 1936.

Root, M. B.: What the Probation Officer Can Do for Special Types of Offenders, *Federal Probation,* (December, 1949), pp. 36–46.

Routzahn, Mary S. and Louisa Wilson: Public Understanding of Probation, *Federal Probation,* Vol. 7, (1943), pp. 14–17.

Rubin, Sol: Adult Parole Systems in the United States, National Probation and Parole Association, 1949, *Supplement,* 1956.

——A Legal View of Probation and Parole Conditions, *National Probation and Parole Association Journal* (January, 1956), pp. 33–37.

Rumney, Jay and Joseph P. Murphy: *Probation and Social Adjustment,* New Brunswick, N. J. Rutgers University Press, 1952.

Rusche, George, and Otto Kirchheimer: *Punishment and Social Structure,* New York: Columbia University Press, 1939.

Sanson, Don R.: Techniques in Probation Supervision, *Probation* New York, Vol. 20, (1942), pp. 71–77.

—— Probation and Parole for the Misdemeanant, *National Probation and Parole Association Journal,* 1949, pp. 186–192.

Sanders, Barkev S.: Testing Parole Prediction, *Proceedings,* American Prison Association, 1935.

Schmideberg, M.: The Parole Reports, *Focus,* (Jan, 1950), pp. 12–15.

Schnur, A. C.: Predicting Parole Outcome, *Focus,* (May 1949), pp. 70–75.

——: The Validity of Parole Selection, *Social Forces,* Vol. 29, (1951) pp. 322–328.

Schramm, Gustav L.: Developing Probation as a Profession, *National Probation and Parole Association Yearbook,* (1936), pp. 298–308.

Schroeder, Paul L.: Probation and the Court-Clinic Relationship, *Proceedings,* American Prison Association, (1936), pp. 81–85.

Schuessler, K. F.: Parole Prediction: Its History and Status, *Journal of Criminal Law and Criminology* Vol. 45, (Nov-Dec, 1954), pp. 425–431.

Schwartz, R.: Prediction of Parole in Prisons, *Federal Probation,* (March, 1949), pp. 36–41.

Scott, A. W., Jr.: The Pardoning Power, *Annals,* (Nov, 1952), pp. 95–100.

Scudder, K. J.: Prisons Will Not Solve our Crime Problem, *Federal Probation,* (March, 1954). pp, 32–39.

Sellin, Thorsten: Probation and Parole, *Encyclopaedia of the Social Sciences,* New York, Macmillan, 1935, Vol. VII, pp. 435–439.

——Probation and Parole in Sweden, National Probation and Parole Association *Yearbook,* 1949, pp. 249–551.

Selling, Lowell S.: The Psychiatrist and the Probation Officer, National Probation and Parole Association *Yearbook,* 1936, pp. 266–279.

Sharp, L. J.: Inservice Training in Probation and Parole, *Federal Probation* (December, 1951), pp. 25–30.

Shulman, Harry M.: Group Work—A New Program for Probation, National Probation and Parole Association, *Yearbook,* (1939), pp. 116–129.

Silverman, E.: Surveillance, Treatment and Casework Supervision, *National Probation and Parole Association,* (January, 1956), pp. 22–26.

Smith, E. R.: Supervision of Field Personnel, *National Probation and Parole Association,* (1953), pp. 79–85.

Smith, P. A.: Principal Criteria for Evaluating Parole Progress, *National Probation and Parole Association,* (1953), pp. 38–42.

Smyth, G. W.: The Destiny of Probation and Parole, *American Prison Association,* (1951), pp. 141–52.

Sobeloff, S. E.: Parole is Here to Stay, *Federal Probation,* (Dec, 1954), pp. 6–9.

Stanley, F. G.: Attracting Employer Interest in Parolees, *Focus,* (July, 1950), pp. 102–105.

Stern, L. T.: Popular or Scientific Evaluation of Probation and Parole, *National Probation and Parole Association,* (1948), pp. 55–70.

Sterne, R. S.: *Outcome of Parole as Related to Pre-Parole Prognosis,* Pennsylvania Committee on Penal Affairs, 1946.

Stone, W. T.: Administrative Aspects of the Special Intensive Parole Program, *Proceedings of American Correctional Association,* 1956, pp. 126–131.

Stukert, William L.: Publicizing Probation, *Proceedings, American Prison Association,* 1939, pp. 113–121.

Sullivan, K.: *Girls on Parole,* New York, Houghton, Miffling Co. 1955.

——Are Parolee Convicts a Danger to You? *Woman's Home Companion,* (January, 1950).

Sutherland, E. H. and Donald R. Cressey: *Principles of Criminology,* (6th ed.) Philadelphia, Lippincott, 1956.

Tabb, B. I. and Podair, S.: Group Education with Parolees, *Federal Probation,* (Sept, 1954), pp. 33–37.

Taber, Robert C.: The Value of Case Work to the Probationer, *National Probation and Parole Association Yearbook,* 1940, pp. 167–179.

Taft, Donald R.: *Criminology,* New York: Macmillan, 1947.

Tappan. Paul W.: *Juvenile Delinquency,* New York: McGraw-Hill, 1949.

——*Contemporary Correction,* New York: McGraw-Hill, 1951.

——The Legal Rights of Prisoners, *Annals,* (May, 1954), pp. 99–111.

——*Crime, Justice and Correction,* New York: McGraw-Hill, 1960.

Teeters, Negley K.: *Penology from Panama to Cape Horn,* Philadelphia: Univ. of Pennsylvania Press, 1946.

Tibbitts, Clark: Success or Failure on Parole can be Predicted, *Journal of Criminal Law and Criminology,* (May, 1931).

Timasheff, Nicholas S.: *One Hunderd Years of Probation,* New York: Fordham University Press, 1941.

——Probation and Imposed Peace, *Thought,* Fordham University *Quarterly,* Vol 16, (1941), pp. 275–296.

——*Probation in the Light of Criminal Statistics,* New York: The Declan X. McMullen Company, Inc., 1949.

Tompkins, Dorothy Culver: *Sources for the Administration of Criminal Justice,* Sacramento, Calif.; Special Crime Study Commissions and California State Board of Corrections, 1949.

Travers, P.: Experiment in the Supervision of Parole Offenders Addicted to Narcotic Drugs, *American Journal of Correction,* (March-April, 1957) pp. 4–7.

Trecker, Harleigh B.: The Use of Community Agencies in Probation Work, *Federal Probation,* Vol. 11, (1947), pp. 21–28.

——Social Work Principles in Probation, *Federal Probation,* (March, 1955).

Trought, Thomas William: *Probation in Europe,* Oxford: Basil Blackwood, 1927.

b206

Union of South Africa, Penal and Prison Reform Commission, 1947 Report (U.G. No. 47–'47) Pretoria: Gov't Printer, 1947.

United Kingdom: Departmental Committee on the *Probation of Offenders Act,* 1907. *Report* (Cmd. 5001) London: H. M. Stationery Office, 1909.

——Departmental Committee on the Training, Appointment and Payment of Probation Officers. *Report.* (Cmd. 1601) London: H. M. Stationery Office, 1922.

——Departmental Committee on the Treatment of Young Offenders *Report* (Cmd. 2831) London: H. M. Stationery Office, 1927.

——Departmental Committee on the Social Services in Courts of Summary Judisdiction. *Report* (Cmd. 5122) London: H. M. Stationery Office, 1936.

——Departmental Committee on the Care of Children. *Report* (Cmd.6922) London: H. M. Stationery Office, 1946.

United Nations: Probation and Related Measures, Department of Social Affairs, 1951.

——*Parole and After-Care,* Department of Social Affairs. 1954.

——*Practical Results and Financial Aspects of Adult Probation in Selected Countries,* Department of Social Affairs, 1954.

United Prison Association of Mass.: What's New in Parole. *Correctional Research,* (January, 1953).

United States of America: Attorney General's Advisory Committee on Crime *Annotated Bibliography on Probation,* compiled by Caroline S. Hughes Washington, D. C.: Dept. of Justice, 1937, (mimeograph).

——Department of Justice. The Attorney General's Survey of Release Procedures, Vol. 1, Digest of Federal and State Laws of Release Procedures, Vol. II, *Probation,* Washington, D. C. Government Printing Office, 1939.

——National Commission on Law Observance and Enforcement, *Report on Penal Institutions,* Probation and Parole Report No. 9 Washington D. C., Government Printing Office, 1931.

——Attorney General's *Survey* Probation, Pardons, Parole. Washington, D. C., Government Printing Office, 1940.

United States Board of Parole: *Annual Reports.*

Van Waters, M.: The Tapering-off Process from Institution to Community Living, *American Prison Association,* (1950), pp. 134–137.

Vaught, B.: Probation and Parole from the Judge's Point of View, *Federal Probation,* (December, 1954), pp. 3–5.

Vinter, Robert D. and Morris, Janowitz: *Comparative Study of Juvenile Correctional Institutions: A Research Report,* December, 1961, (mimeograph). Ann Arbor, University of Michigan School of Social Work.

Vold, George B.: *Prediction Methods and Parole,* (Hanover, N. H. Sociological Press, 1931); also, Do Parole Prediction Tables Work In Practice? in Publications of the *American Sociological Society,* 1931.

——*Theoretical Criminology,* Prediction of Delinquency, New York: Oxford University Press, 1958, pp. 131–135.

Vedder, Clyde B.: *Juvenile Offenders,* Springfield, Illinois: Charles C Thomas, Publisher, 1963, Chapters, Probation, and Parole Supervision.

Wallace, J.: The Casework Approach to Rules, National Probation and Parole Association, (Jan., 1956), pp. 14–21.

Wallack, W. M. and J. Sheedy: The Service Unit as Part of the Prison Program, *Prison World,* (Nov-Dec, 1948; also Jan-Feb, 1949).

Ward, Frederick, Jr.: Probation Officer as a Leader in Community Organization, *Federal Probation,* Vol. 10, (1946), pp. 30–34.

Wagner, Allan H.: *Probation: A Selected Bibliography on the Individualized Treatment of the Offender,* New York: Russell Sage Foundation, 1948.

Warner, S. B.: Factors Determining Parole from the Massachusetts Reformatory, *Journal of Criminal Law and Criminology,* (August, 1923).

Weiffenbach, Milton: An Approach to Presentence Investigation, National Probation and Parole Association *Yearbook,* (1942), pp. 165–176.

Weinberg, S. K.: Theories of Criminality and Problems of Prediction, *Journal of Criminal Law and Criminology,* Vol. 45, (Nov-Dec, 1954), pp. 412–424.

Weiss, M. H. and H. A. Rikelman: A Cooperative Effort in Finding Jobs for Prisoners, *Correction,* New York, (June, 1953), pp. 19–23.

Weller, Miriam D.: The Development of the Federal Probation System, *Social Service Review,* Chicago, Vol. 18, (1944), pp. 42–58.

White, R. Clyde: State Administration of Adult Probation and Parole, *Federal Probation,* Vol. 5, (1941), pp. 14–16.

Williams, M. E.: Developing Employment Opportunities for Parolees, *Focus,* (March, 1952), pp. 47–51.

Williamson, Margaretta A.: *The Social Worker in the Prevention and Treatment of Delinquency,* New York. Columbia University Press, 1935.

Wilson, D. J.: Should We Employ Ex-prisoners? *Canadian Business,* (April, 1952).

Wilson, Everett E.: The Nature of Probation, *Social Service Review,* Chicago, Vol. 20, (1946), pp. 396–402.

Witmer, Helen L.: Social Case Work in the Field of Juvenile Probation, National Probation and Parole Association *Yearbook,* (1941), pp. 153–166.

Wise, R. E.: Parole Progress, *National Probation and Parole Association,* (1950), pp. 111–120.

Wollan, Kenneth I.: The Use of Group Activity in Probation Work, National Probation and Parole Association, *Yearbook.* (1958), pp. 240–255.

Wood, Arthur Evans, and John Barker Waite: *Crime and its Treatment: Social and Legal Aspects of Criminology,* New York: American Book Co., 1941.

Wood, A. L.: The Alternatives of the Death Penalty, *Annals:* (Nov, 1952), pp. 63–72.

Wylegala, Victor B.: Re-judgment Investigation of the Delinquent, in Association of Juvenile Court Judges of America, *Proceedings* (1940), pp. 15–21.

Young, Pauline V.: *Interviewing in Social Work*: *A Sociological Analysis* New York: McGraw-Hill, 1935.

——Social Treatment in Probation and Delinquency: Treatise and Casebook for Court Workers, Probation Officers and Other Child Welfare Workers New York: McGraw-Hill, 1937.

Young, Pauline V.: (ed.) *Principles and Methods of Probation; Selected Readings, Case Materials, Study Outlines and Bibliography for the Study of Adult and Juvenile Probation,* Los Angeles: Western Educational Service, 1935.

——*Social Treatment in Probation and Delinquency,* New York: McGraw-Hill, 1952, (rev. ed.) .

Yount, P. D.: A Compilation of Criteria for Parole Selection, *Proceedings of American Prison Association,* (1948) , pp. 280–286.

Zeigler, Edwin B.: Pre-sentence and Pre-parole Investigation, *National Probation and Parole Association, Yearbook,* (1946) , pp. 154–163.